THE UNSI

ABDUL SAMAD HAIDARI

عبدالصمد حیدری

What resonates with me the most in
Abdul Samad Haidari's poetry is not
just how he employs words to challenge
a system designed to oppress and strip
away his identity and dignity; it's also how
he creates beauty within the context of
tragedy, symbolising strength and inspiring
empowerment for resistance.

Behrouz Boochani
Human rights defender, writer and film producer.
Author of *No Friend But the Mountains* (Picador
2018) and *Freedom, Only Freedom* (Bloomsbury
2023).

———

In *The Unsent Condolences* each and every
poem builds the unconquered fortress within
the human who has endured the atrocities
of evil. Abdul Samad Haidari's erudite vision
reverberates our hearts, harmonises our
minds, ignites our humanity to stand up and
take action. In our history, there are only
a few poems that have inspired marches
against injustice, here we have an entire
collection.

Angela Costi
Poet and social justice advocate.
Author of *An Embroidery of Old Maps
and New* (Spinifex Press 2021).

———

Abdul Samad Haidari is a writer whose poetry tells a very personal and yet somehow universal story of belonging, injustice, uprootedness and loss. For anyone wanting to really understand what it can mean to be forced to flee home, family and country, Haidari's poems are recommended reading.

Prof. Erika Feller

Former Assistant High Commissioner for Protection with the United Nations High Commissioner for Refugees.

———

Abdul Samad Haidari's *Unsent Condolences* rewards sustained reflection one poem, or one series of poems at a time. Woven around Persian proverbs, Haidari's words echo the rich cadences and reflect the vivid imagery of the language, land and culture into which he was born. Childhood memories of goodness and love fade to bewilderment as scenes of war tell the poet's story, shadowing the sunlit morning with violence and suffering, death and fear.

Deborah Storie

Peace-builder and Baptist Pastor, who has lived in and worked on community development and peace-building projects in Afghanistan.

———

ISBN 978-0-6455881-3-2
Typeface: Tiempos (Klim) Production: Ian Robertson Printing: IngramSpark
For additional information, bulk or educational purchases, and other resources,
please contact Paul Komesaroff / Ethica Projects Pty Ltd
paul.komesaroff@monash.edu

www.palaver.com
Palaver is an imprint of Ethica Projects Pty Ltd
10 Barnato Grove Armadale Victoria 3143 Australia

THE UNSENT CONDOLENCES

—

ABDUL SAMAD HAIDARI

عبدالصمد حیدری

Author of *The Red Ribbon*
(2019)

I AM NOT UPROOTED, AND I AM NOT SILENCED.
I AM ENGAGED, REMAIN CURIOUS, AND FIRM.
I AM UTTERLY PREPARED.
I RELATE TO ALL TIME AND SPACE.
I AM ALL YOU SEEK.
I AM ALL YOU NEED.

FOR

My enchanting grandmother
Mai Jan Haidari

My courageous grandfather
Malik Ghulam Haidar Khan Haidari

My moonstone, Ammi Jan
Amir Bigum Haidari

My beloved father
Malik Yazdan Haidari

The shimmering moon, my foster-mother
Pam Dunn
New Zealand High Commissioner
to Malaysia and Brunei Darussalam

The loving soul, my foster-father
Dr Te Manawa Murray Dunn

The blooming stars of my life
My endearing siblings

The editor of this book,
the symbol of light
Lesmina Sari

To all suspended stars, the refugees across the world,
particularly refugees in Indonesia.
You have every right to exist and exist fully.
You are as important as the nature around us.

To all women across the planet,
especially women of my homeland, Afghanistan,
through whom men came into existence
and learned the language of love.

Table of Contents

ما از بـی کفنی زنده ایم

V — WE ARE ALIVE ...

من آنجا ریشـه در خاک دارم

VI — I HAVE ROOTS / IN THE SOIL THERE

Foreword
Raimond Gaita

The cries of pain in this book will sear your heart and conscience. You may sometimes not be able to keep reading Abdul Samad Haidari's poems. His collection offers little place of rest from its unrelenting, sometimes despairing, efforts to make its readers understand the meaning of the pain it depicts.

Simone Weil, the French philosopher, calls the pain Abdul Samad Haidari describes 'affliction' which she distinguishes from even very great suffering that does not have an inseparable element of degradation. Abdul suffered it in many forms: as an individual who has been the victim of wanton, sometimes sadistic, cruelty; as a refugee condemned to wander the world often without social standing or respect; and as a Hazara, a member of a minority ethnic group that is the target of denigration and persecution, which Abdul calls genocide because their murderers judged them to be unfit to inhabit the earth.

But you will be grateful to Abdul for his unsparing efforts to make you understand the meaning of affliction fully rather than partially as we usually do when we contemplate the suffering of refugees — to understand in your bones rather than only in your head. Grateful, because as Australians we should know that our governments have shamed us with their ruthlessly devised and enforced policy against refugees fleeing their homes by land and sea. Had we understood what Abdul tries to make us understand no government would have dared implement those policies.

Abdul is often incredulous that human beings could do to other human beings what they have done to him and to others on behalf of whom he speaks. With an intensity enhanced and disciplined by the gift of poetry he calls for our compassion, but also for something more important. Or, to put it more precisely, he calls for compassion and outrage, transformed by the realisation that the affront to his human dignity is a violation of the miracle that is every human life. His heart-rending bewilderment is in a key tuned to the violation of something inalienably precious. In these poems it causes even nature to weep for him and for humanity because of evil we do to one another.

We need art to enable us to understand these things. Of the literary arts, poetry does it best. As guardians of the natural languages in which they find their voices poets (to adapt the words of Ezra Pound) are the antennae of humanity, finely attuned to good and evil.

Abdul speaks in many voices, but the voice of hope is faint. Not the voice that cries for justice, however. The wonder of this book — the deepest reasons why it is a gift — is that it does not allow our outrage at justice shamelessly affronted to make us doubt or despair of justice itself. It takes our outrage to an ethical space where we can affirm even more strongly and surely our sense of the need for justice if we are to honour our humanity.

July 2023
Melbourne

Raimond Gaita is honorary professorial fellow in the Melbourne Law School and emeritus professor of Moral Philosophy at King's College London. His numerous books include *Good and Evil: An Absolute Conception* (Routledge 1989); *Romulus, My Father* (Text 1998); *A Common Humanity: Thinking About Love & Truth & Justice* (Routledge 1999); and *Justice and Hope: Lectures Essays and Other Writings* (MUP 2023).

Preface
Abdul Samad Haidari

I opened my eyes in a mud-made castle, in a small village known as Dahmardah-e-Gulzar. Dahmardah is situated in Arghandab region of Northern Zabul province, Afghanistan. My birth was marked by the conduct of a systematic annihilation, genocide. The perpetrators of this heinous act were none other than the same turbaned colonisers who had long ago unjustly confiscated a substantial portion of our ancestral lands, the lands of the Hazaras who existed in Afghanistan prior to the magnificent Buddhas of Bamiyan whose grandeur adorned the landscape.

As a Hazara child, I witnessed my people entangled in the intricate web of an historical injustice that has continued to reverberate through the generations. As the wind of war exploded, it carried me away from my homeland. I was forced to undertake an arduous journey that led me to the unfamiliar terrain of a construction site in Tehran, Iran. Instead of finding solace and security, I was thrust into the depths of an unforgiving reality where I was subjected to the dehumanising conditions of child labour — a cruel existence akin to slavery. There, the grandchildren of Saadi and Hafiz, held me captive and made me learn a new and an unfamiliar term 'refugee' — another name for the start of struggle, the end of existence.

Unsurprisingly, I was not of the first generation to become a refugee. My family experienced this bitter reality for five generations. I was forced to spend a significant amount of my life until now separated from my parents. The weight of this prolonged separation like an ever-present companion, has undoubtedly left indelible imprints upon my soul. However, my experiences and sharp pen brought me back to the soil of my ancestors, reclaiming a connection to my roots. In 2007, my lifelong passion for journalism came to fruition as I took a leap into a fascinating world, embracing the sweet world of ink and paper. I seized the opportunity to work with two influential media outlets, *The Daily Outlook Afghanistan* group of newspapers and later *The Daily Afghanistan Express*.

As my name started to circulate across the country, those same turbaned men with holes in their trousers along with political, religious groups and warlords grew increasingly uncomfortable because I asked them some more questions and published more answers. Unable to swallow my words, they orchestrated a campaign to silence me, forcing me to abandon everything I had built from scratch and seek safety elsewhere. I ended up in Indonesia, where nearly ten most precious years of my life were stolen — in a place, both sanctuary and prison, where thousands of refugees like myself were caught in the border wars and held hostage. Its borders, like invisible walls, confined me to the margins of society denying me the freedom to build anew.

The border wars raged on and I remained caught in their merciless grip. But amidst the darkness, a flicker of light emerged from within me — the firm determination to reclaim my dignity, challenge the circumstances that sought to define me. In that state of defiance, I discovered solace and empowerment in the art of poetry after I lost my voice for the second time because of my status as a refugee. I wrote as a life-giving form of resistance to the torturous treatment and slow deaths endured by my fellow refugees and to the ongoing genocide of my Hazara people and the destruction of our life and culture. The effort in my writing was to offer stark truths and profound reflections that open space for remembrance and reconstruction, highlighting the strengths, richness and beauty of Hazaragi history as the indigenous people of Afghanistan — a history marred by confiscated lands, shattered families and stolen lives.

Against all odds, systemic political pressures, limitation of resources and the denial of the right to sign a contract, I emerged as the first refugee in Indonesia to publish my first book, *The Red Ribbon*, in 2019. This illustrated book of poetry, despite the countless barriers and obstacles I faced, became one of the top three best-selling books in Indonesia in both 2020 and 2021. My effort was to capture the raw emotions and untold narratives that lay hidden in the hearts of refugees, the anguish felt and the untold stories of those who have tragically lost their lives within those desolate spaces as a result of psychological and physical pressures.

The Unsent Condolences is my second poetry book. It is about our life, buried in the cold rifts of camps with no access to basic human rights. We begged, we cried, we wrote and yet everyone stood silent, watched us perish bit by bit with no media or nation stepping forward. The entire world turned against us, media hid our death toll and some even confronted us burying our fellows in their moist soil because of our religious beliefs. They pushed us against the cold walls and the walls pushed us back to earth until every bit of us crashed. They mistreated and tore us apart from our loved ones for more than ten fatal years. They put locks on our tongues, stole our natural human rights and laughed at our death with joy and arrogance. Those countries and institutions who pretended to help caused more harms — sold bits of our lungs, our wrinkled skin and fingernails for cash. These entities campaigned for dollars, displaying our raw flesh on their banners and reports like henna leaves, green from outside, raw meat from within. They did it very thoroughly and those countries who funded that project are steeped in our blood up to their necks. Their incarcerating camps are bursting with the fragrance of our youthful blood. Our drops of blood and tears are still running across their camps as our bare skulls thump against their walls. I smelt blood when I opened my window in the morning or walked in the rain in the evening. Those who held our hands, sold our tears. They've nothing left of us, except the extracted pieces of our hearts in their tyrant walls of stone. We have grown tired of praising the exotic flowers.

Yet, in the journey of re-gaining my full existence as one of the children of this soil, I keep counting seconds with every breath that remains in my chest to celebrate the sweet hours of reunion with my aged mother and my siblings — whom I have been banned from seeing for more than nine fatal years.

I am yearning for my fragments to be welded, put back in place so life forms a full meaning — for I know I won't be able to travel this long and curving road alone. I am running out of lungs, rotating in the rings of earth — nights without laughter around the *sufra* of warm *naan* and *chai*; mornings, the stories of a lonesome moon, missing the smiles of soothing stars. All the wanderlusts drowned in the extended gaps of my footprints. I am bitterly exhausted and want my flesh that was removed from my ribs to be re-wrapped around my rotten bones so my fading visions regain the strength to regrow and my chest to be whole. Therein, I will grow old in the warmth of an ever-lasting home. Home that only knows how to mend and heal.

July 2023
Wellington Aotearoa/New Zealand.

THE UNSENT CONDOLENCES

I
PROLOGUE

Quilt of rhymes

The Unsent Condolences
is not a collection of poems
but parts of me —
is not just words
collated into a quilt of rhymes
but a jar full of fresh scars.

Every word is a hurricane of teardrops,
as mouth failed to moan —
they spilled out of solitude
when the heart
could no longer mourn.

        Every hymn is a portion of my bare lungs,
        cries of digging daggers,
        diving through my stripped bones,
        forgotten across the cold corners.

        Each stroke rested upon the paper,
        sparked flames of hell upon me —
        hefts of pains,
                surging fierce and wild
                as though someone was nailing thorns
                upon my bosom with the edges of axes.

    Blood wailed up,
    the stumps stood thick —
a still river of red
round the frozen surface of my cheeks —
half hidden by the night,
half drowned in the tide.

        My soul collapsed
        like the portrait
        of my home's bombed walls —
        scattered and lifeless,
        weeping in the debris
        buried alive.

/...

This book composes my grief,
thousands of unsent condolences
to a mother with collateral damages
and tears scorched the sore soil —
a composition of striking lyrics,
bouncing against the walls of tyranny
built to cover curvature of stories,
compressed against the roof of my mouth.

December 28, 2022
Pajajaran, Bogor, Indonesia

II

THE RADIANT DAWN IS /
MORE BEAUTIFUL THAN /
A THOUSAND MOONLIT CROWNS

از نـــور علم تو را را چونـ\
صد خانه روشـــن اسـت

"The Radiant Dawn is More Beautiful Than a
Thousand Moonlit Crowns" has deep roots in
Persian proverbs. My grandmother often recited
this proverb, emphasising the transformative
power of education and the wide-reaching impact
it can have on society. The teachings of my and
ancestors and parents — through proverbs, stories
and examples — have profoundly inluenced my
academic path, serving as an important root from
which I have grown. Their wisdom resonates within
me, forming an essential part of my being.

Threads of psalms
To Baba *and* Ammi: *My moonstones*

Your names surge
across my mournful mouth
like threads of psalms,
connecting soul with stars,
flesh with bones;
breath to lungs

> but agony chokes me up,
> unable to formulate fully.

I turn into fog
in the breathless air
that bears the taste of gore,
droplets of forbidden rain —
each part and bit of me
> rolls
> down
> the paper of my torso.

Hands shiver
like broken branches
of my bombed almond trees;
eyes search
> for what arms can't embrace.

Chest wails inwardly,
pining for your tenderness
what hands fail to feel.

When I run to humans,
I encounter piles of rocks;
when I extend my hands for a bandage,
they pour salt.

Their ears,
        two cracked mouths of volcanoes,
eyes,
        burning arrows from hell,
hearts,
        faint tones of the sick,
hands,
        merciless claws of bears
and tongues,
        the smearing swords,
        cutting the earth
into two hundred parts.

No one I ran to
        wiped my tears
but sold instead.

They've stolen the skin
from beneath my feet;
I dab with bare feet —
my toes are red,
city is painted with my blood.

I roam with chest cracked,
my chin has lost shape;
forehead the origin
        with fine lines,
        showcasing the range of borders,
                I braved,
        the depth of seas,
           I sailed.

Silence is full of violence,
desiccated creatures
howl at a dying sun
and cement the sky
to cover a withering moon.

                  /...

Eyes burn from the ashes of death —
every breath I take,
contains powder of blades.

My shoulders heave
under the weight of torments;
I have gone numb,
pushing them on.

They wove a rug from my skin;
gave it to me
to cover myself;
a mat out of my nails
to sleep on.

I live with bare waist,
wounds,
more fragile
than the wings of butterflies.

I feel cold and frozen;
shrink into a tight ball
when the brinish wind blows.

My soul stands instead of me
when they read my number —
paper with a name or address,
mightier than my human identity.

It has been a while now
that I walk under the rain
to wash my wounds
and float in the sea
to mend my cuts.

I wander in the forest
to remove the binds and chains;

escape from masjids, churches
and hide in caves
to seek shelter.

I trance with shadow
to befriend the night;
run to mountains
to escape humankind.

November 17, 2018
Jakarta, Indonesia

I am all you seek

I'm a fragile bud
    on a misty petal,
    pure and innocent —

    an empty page
        to be filled
        with the ink of love.

I'm a seeker of joy
        amid the tarnished world —
a messenger of kindness.

I don't wish spells of genocide
or dark venom of hatred
to stain the pages of my chest.

        I'm a little child,
        arisen through
        the tender womb of light
        like a drift of air,
        cloudless and bright.

I know nothing about religion
nor do I wish to belong to any
or fall behind
the random eyelids of terror.

Childhood is my faith,
let this breathe first —
        no big rosy dreams
        drive my emergent vision
        but to grow and blossom
        in the flourishing gardens
        of two nurturing souls
        in whose hearts
        beats mine.

I don't wish to be shaken by loud bombs
nor do I wish a gun on my face
or a blunt knife at my throat.

       I fear losing oxygen
       like my friend Ali Sina
       neither can I stand the idea
              of missing a pair of legs
              like Khadija.

Stop planting bombs —
powder caused
internal wounds
deep under my skin.

I'm scared of wins and losses.
I've lost the counts and discounts.

       I wish to grow old in the village,
       I opened my eyes;
              pursue life with those
                 whom I spoke first

                 understood me;

       be with those
       who laughed
       when I smiled,
       cried
       when I mourned.

       I can't walk this worn path
without my arms round
the sides of Uzbeks and Turkmens,
       carry the flag high
       without Tajiks;
       smile to the stars
without Pashtuns and Aimaqs,
do *Attan*[1] without Arabs and Pashayis

                        /...

or harvest the wheat in its high fields
without Qizilbashs.

> Hazara, my nickname,
> Baluch, my tribe,
> Pameri, my race,
> Nuristani, my strength,
> Sayyid, my faith;
> humanity, my identity —

I am all,
you seek,
all you need.

> God's hands rose
> with a brushstroke of colours,
> on a canvas of masterpiece:
> I grow black at night,
> brown in the morning,
>> celadon in Spring,
>> green in Summer,
>> yellow in Autumn,
>> white in Winter —

I carry all the colours,
your eyes can behold.

> Too small to judge;
> too delicate to be judged.

> I can't tell who can
but He is certainly loving and kind;
Creative and Forgiving.

Someone Who Resides
beyond the lights
and within our hearts.

October 13, 2016
Cisarua Bogor, Indonesia

———

1. *Attan*: A traditional dance in Afghanistan.

30

Garden of grace

I am not uprooted,
nor silenced.
I exist fully,
relate to all time and space.

I am prepared,
    rising again
    in the bosom
    of a fruitful Summer,
tucked away in-between
every spring and fall.

        I can't deny
        how lovely rising feels
        in the adversity of discovering
        for I mastered,
        touched them all
        in the tranquillity of poems.

I shouldered all morning griefs,
cried with afternoon sunsets,
have known the late evening aftermaths,
heard voices with a dying fall;
cried with eyes that shed blood.

        I never lose myself
        because *Baba*'s[1] words
        abide in me forever —
        I grew up seeing visions
        that fixed me in shared phrases.

When death stares,
I hold the light of *Baba*'s[1] vision,
recite songs of *Ammi*'s[2] springing words;
embrace *Madar Kalan*'s[3] soulful wisdom.

/...

I re-embrace the core of life
as their soothing voices
touch the strings of my heart —
I get enlivened to their embraces,
reaching lovingly towards me
though millions of miles
stand between us.

I dance to the cadence
of my ancestors' breath,
composing rhymes
out of their heartbeats.

Calling their names is a healing,
a prayer and a submission for worship.

October 10, 2014
Bogor, Indonesia

————

1. *Baba*: Father.
2. *Ammi*: Mother.
3. *Madar Kalan*: Grandmother.

Breeze of God

Here,
sights are full of life;
fields wear green grassy gowns;
     there,
     worn-out battlegrounds
     to a thousand forgotten tombs.

Here,
mothers clothed
in soft threads of silk;
     there,
     shrouded,
     stitched out of wrinkled skins.

Here,
air fresh breeze of God,
blows of brilliance;
     there,
     extracted pieces
     from human veins,
     ashes
     with no sign
     or sound of life.

Here,
  water runs in perfect rhythm
  in the bosoms of rivers —
vibrant throbs of mountains,
  tall and tranquil;
     there,
     flood of blood,
     cacophony of rapid rockets;
          sudden screams of horror,
          topping tears of death;
          sunken mountains
          with broken cheeks.

/...

Here,
Flowers, blossom of life;
fragrance,
rich and reviving
      as though another planet is just formed;
      there,
      empty towers of wilted tulips,
      smearing smell of aged blood —
      sinking deep;
      choking life like flood.

Here,
is life,
      there,
      strife.

Here,
religion,
brotherhood and peace,
      there,
      war and disease.

Here,
winds,
rhymes of laughter,
      there,
      sad moans of bombs.

Here,
sky pours rain,
      there,
      dust and pain.

Here,
clouds,
dewdrops of seas,
      there,
      smoke of explosions
      and burned trees.

Here,
children's laughter,
best songs of birds,
      there,
      shivering echoes of fear
      and colliding clouds.

Here,
culprits in prison,
      there,
      the victims.

Here,
women empowered,
running a nation,
      there,
      women dragged down;
      forced to run the kitchens.

Here,
people build schools,
      there,
      exploded and bombed.

Here,
people celebrate life,
      there,
      death and grief.

/...

Here,
streets smell love,
      there,
            thick smoke of shroud.

Here,
justice flourishes for free,
there revenge replaces forgiveness
and peace bows down on knees.

January 06, 2017
Cisarua, Bogor, Indonesia

Pathos of separation
From my mother

Once again
the cold winter has arrived,
carrying with it your childhood fragrance
from behind the reefs of mountains,
wrapped in frozen petals of snowflakes
yet you did not come.

Winter has gone by,
the reviving Spring is here;
aromatic flowers are back to life
yet you did not come.

Spring has sung its farewell,
the rewarding Summer too;
Autumn has brought nothing
except the innocent memories of you
yet you did not come.

My eyes have glazed over
with these long delays,
hair has turned white;
my vision sees nothing
except the dark sight of night.

And yet
I still keep the windows open,
waiting for the clatter of your shoes —
my yearning ears hear nothing
but the cold swishing sound
of falling leaves,
raging over the doorsteps
like a tidal wave,
awakened from a groaning sea.

/...

I run towards the door
like a heart–sick fool,
thinking that you are there —
only to encounter
an empty, frosty air.

Your cheerful childhood chants
ring in my head —
like the droplets of rain
and the longing for reunion
is turning me blind.

Tell them to untie
the threads of air
and stop extracting
flesh from bones —
for the swords of tyranny
reached the bones of motherhood.

March 06, 2016
Cisarua, Bogor, Indonesia

III
THE SKY AFAR / EARTH ROUGH

آسمان دور\
ز مین ســـخت

The proverb "The Sky Afar, Earth Rough" finds its origins deeply embedded within the Hazaragi culture. I remember hearing this proverb from my grandparent and parents — notably during the 1990s when the Taliban surrounded Dahmardah from all sides, leaving no viable escape route. This period of colonisation witnessed the village's tragic transformation into an abandoned cemetery of unreported crimes.

Troops of rented boars

Charm of light
grows thinner and weak;
dimming valleys of darkness
sway over the grey fields
like stalking vampires.

Wind heaves with desolate moans,
winter veils the farmlands in white;
trees stand dressed
like exalted brides.

Bushes bow down
      to host the snow;
      snow grooms the bushes
      into Christmas trees.

Freezing breeze rushes,
licking the wooden window
like the whizzy bullets,
whispering the arrival
of rented boars
and I stand behind it,
holding my breath tight
beneath my broken limbs.

Chants of rented boars
shoot high in the air,
loud and clear
like arrows of death —
Allaho Akbar[1] stands alone,
echoing across the dream-land of legends
and ruins life with all its flame.

It goes on and on,
reaching every ear
that yearns for peace,

every synapse
that fires to stay intact.

They are scattered across *Kotali Rasnah*[2]
as troops of lice on your shoulders
when a comb runs through your hair.

They roar closer,
rushing downwards to Bazar
with dirty vehicles and windscreens
covered by thick gore and ashes,
    ascended out of a slaughterhouse.

Some are standing at the back of their Hilux
with long scary beards swaying in the breeze
reminding me of *Madar Kalan*'s home-made brooms,
created out of local bushes.

When the Hilux speeds through puddles,
big black and white turbans
pop-up like rabbits.

Some fall off their heads,
rolling like popcorns
or our goats' manure.

Hilux vehicles sprouting white flags —
two at the front;
two held at the back.

Machine guns and loudspeakers
up on roof tops,
shouting
Taliban zinda bad.
Long live the Taliban.

They march in the village;
some head down to *madrasa*[3]
and some to *Khanju*[4]

/...

searching house to house,
Kalashnikovs,
their necklace of carnage;
rockets rank their shanks.

They hunt down adults,
forcing them to submit,
elders are ejected —
'a waste of space'.

Women are silenced,
shut off,
guns on their heads;
Sharia Law is enforced
to carry out the slow grindings.

Mothers hush children
to fall asleep with Taliban's myth.
I will call the Taliban
if you don't go to sleep.

Dahmardah[5] poses a scary face,
the face of a stranger —
commanding to run.

Residents whose stories of unbeatable bravery
chuckled in every ear across Hazaragi lands,
now seek refuge in mountains —
life is a race and death, cold.

Karlus[6], a groomed dog,
a Taliban sympathiser
barks at every leaf,
shaken by the wind.

Some are disappeared —
      unknown

to be dead
or alive.

Dahmardah turned into
a cold cemetery.
Horror slows breathing down.

My vision bears nothing
except the piles of blundered hearts —
salted and stinky fish
recalls the memory
of rotten human flesh
with oily bones,
dumped in *Kandi Pusht*[7].

I survived the genocide
but how should I survive the traumas?

November 17, 2018
Cisarua, Bogor, Indonesia

—

1 *Allaho Akbar*: Allah is great.
2. *Kotali Rasnah*: The name of a mountain pass that joins Dahmardah with its
   neighbouring area called Rasnah.
3. *Madrasa*: The institution of higher education in the Islamic sciences.
4. *Khanju*: The name of one of the areas in Dahmardah.
5. *Dahmardah*: My birthplace where the glorious orchards were full of vibrant
   dreams, the magnificent mountains stood tall as God's height, and the rivers
   flew like veins, singing in rhymes as though God and nature were in an
   eternal dialogue about life.
6. *Karlus:* An individual who sympathised with the Taliban and actively
   participated in their campaign of torturing, humiliating, and abusing the very
   existence of the Hazara people during the 1990s.
7. *Kandi Pusht*: A place located in Zabul province of Afghanistan where the
   Taliban and locals in the 1990s murdered thousands of Hazara people.

Woozy moans of saxophones

The sun hangs down,
the red-woven of soft lights
drown like a bleeding heart
on the sobbing breath
of Dahmardah's promising highlands.

Grey throne of *Kohizardag*[1]
wears upon his loving shoulders
the late farewell colours of crimson,
showcasing the ominous droplets of steels,
pouring down the freshly dressed roofs
amidst the strikes of Hazara cleansing.

30 minutes later,
when the darkness fully scatters
filling every crack and hole,
isolated echoes of gunshots, *taq, doom, taq*
declare the beginning of a doomsday,
the tyrant whims of carnage —
the start of struggles,
the end of life.

Blazing rays of machineguns,
rushing streams of iron
from *Bukhchijai*'s[2] site
sail in isolated colours of gold —

drowsed tint of purple.

Blond rockets take flight,
falling off at the feet of hillsides,
heaving down in thousands of fragments
as if the moon has crushed.

Ammi's eyes revolve in storms of terror
at every twisting blast of flames,

jumping right and left
with no sign or sound of life —
dread scenes of terror fill her eyes
as though this is our last moment.

Orchestra of grieving cries
explode loud
and vicious
as the waged war stretches on,
reaches every mud-made house,
burns every wood-wrapped roof —
every gasping soul clings to dust
and human bones scream for flesh.

On the scorched ground,
some are curtained,
framed eerily behind rivers of fire;
children scream,
melting like strands of tyres.

Groans and shelling sounds collide,
ringing back-and-forth,
composing a thousand beats
of choked-out synths
like the woozy moans of saxophones,
lamenting on a funeral
in the late hours of evening.

I stand still,
ears engraved by ashes;
crashing waves of terror
and loud screams of valleys —

dead nor alive.

Warm breeze of war
throbs under my skin;

/...

forces my feet to pull
off the tar
and run with ashes of war
on my skin,
bitter cast of gunpowder
in my hair,

searching for a hole
around quiet corners,
in cold cracks of rocks
to hide
and bind my broken bones.

I become sand castles
across the agonised deserts,
raindrop on borderlands;
fish in the realms of dark seas —

each time bargaining
over my soul
to stay attached —
never knowing
if a cruel wind
would blow the light
off my eyes.

I had to leave no traces,
pick my shattered heart up;
jig-saw them back together

and run on —
on bare feet,
holding close bits and pieces
in my pounded palms —

like a bomb defuser
without a helmet
or a racer
without legs.

As I crossed the first landmine,
I saw surgeons lined up
with sharp knives —

                between the heaps of sea salt,
                  on top of hillsides;
            in red painted camps
            to chop off the arms
      that raced with sharks,
      slice off the head
      that bullets missed.

Me,
now floating between
a thousand traces of times
to survive the surgeons
and make friendship with stones
to teach them speak in rhymes.

December 10, 2018
Cisarua, Bogor, Indonesia

———

1. *Kohizardag*: One of the mountains in my birthplace, Dahmardah.
2. *Bukhchijai*: One of the areas in Dahmardah.

The dead flame plays with ash

Darkness stretches its wings,
blazing bullets of machineguns,
dive low on the wrinkled ground,
containing the fragrance of blood.

My heart lies out of my chest,
slayed into two
under the conical fires,
Ammi panics more than the shivering walls
as everyone runs for safety.

Some grab their kids,
some rush without heartbeats.

Children scream,
running in unending circles
across the smoky fields.

Baba runs in one direction,
Ammi to another —
Abdul Ahad down to the ditch,
I, after *Ammi* into swarms of *booltarghina* [1].

Ammi falls on her knees,
stands and gears up again
until we make our way
into a long trench,

pushing us further
into the chest of a tunnel,
where a sense of safety
captures our worn-out eyes.

But terror keeps uprooting
as each rocket and missile lands;

dust falls on our heads
and the scorched earth shakes
as if God of Adam is dead.

Run, *Ammi* cries,
heading to the basement
as the tunnel wounds widen,
pouring on us dust of guns.

We shelter alongside the cattle,
shuddering deeply at rockets' sparks,
calling upon death to survive the gods.

> Beams of weapons
> flash around brightens,
> > blushing the dim lantern
> > that dies down
> > like a fading hope.

> Smell is intense as ammonia;
> fighters' shuffling sound of feet,
> heave outside
> like the hooves of wild horses
> and the shooting sounds of guns,
> burst into extended sighs.

> > Death is creeping at every inch.
> > It is at the front door,
> > poking through the cracks of walls
> > from beneath the shackles in my chest.

Madar Kalan weeps but slowly,
putting her rough palm to her mouth
to choke her moans;
her voice suffocates within her
and fades away in low-pitched tones.

/...

Echoes of loud sounds slow down
as the psalms of ascending morning
crack upon a rooster's heart.

No bird sings the next day,
rampage dirges at every house
        and emptiness stands in grey.

Trees are wounded,
wearing smoky gowns
as if they are baked
and with farms of ashes
alone to capture.

February 21, 2013
Kabul, Afghanistan

———

1. *Booltarghina*: A local bush that grows in Dahmardah. It is light cyan
   in colour and huge with fluffy feathers.

Debris of red flower buds

In loving memory of my sister, Hakima Haidari

Her eyes were open,
wide and unguarded in debris,
beneath the small arc,
between the two melting hills,
dimming away
like a twinkling candle
as the fireflies of war
exploded into thunders.

Ashes fell in furious flows,
enclosing the cords of her heart
each time
her lungs gasped
for a last breath.

Her chest was stamped
by darts of hatred;
the holes sighed verses of God
with each drop of blood,
sprung through her mouth;

her fractured forehead
two enflamed fountains,
cheeks, the red flower buds,
blossomed in Autumn.

Blazing ground held her low,
seeping every drop of gore
raced out of bullet-holes
across the summoned soil —
her blood lent its colour
to the withered ground.

/...

51

I rushed to catch the falling roses
but they started losing their charms
faster than the field could count
and I only embraced sticky ashes,
red and an oily ribbon —
a gift of faded rose,
wrapped in the oily pouch
of raging war.

A delicate rose
from the garden of angels,
burst into a hundred cherries —
incised flesh of grey,
married the dust.

You would feel the flames
running through your veins
if you looked into her eyes.

January 21, 2019
Jakarta, Indonesia

Death's clatter

Winter runs long and cold,
hunger digs beds —
rugged and sore.

White,
spooky flags pierce the sky,
long-bearded men,
wearing thick kohl
in black turbans,

headlong in dented roadways,
proclaiming victory
over Hazaras —
death's clatter rings near tonight.

Their venomous chants
and copper-snake breath,
suckle my ears
like the blistering arrows.

They carry weapons bigger than me —
firm and determined,
bearing on their foreheads
slopes of battered graves —
death's clatter rings near tonight.

There is a flood of dewdrops in eyes,
drought of *Karbala*[1] in mouth —
feet are swollen;
soul quivers
under the edge of swords —
death's clatter rings near tonight.

Kitchen is sad and silent,
no fresh fragrance of warm *naan*
beats through the empty *tandoor.*

/...

53

No pennant of firewood smoke
runs through the chimneys
of mud-made houses.

Our bellies are full of thunders
over the empty cloth of wheat-lot,
hanging in the kitchen —
death's clatter rings near tonight.

The black bears search for human roots
in the yellow and brown-leaved
farmlands of corn and almonds.

They have locked our paths,
shut the time and space;
we hold on to the tails of genocide —
death's clatter rings near tonight.

No clothes to keep us warm in the winter breeze,
no medication to press against the wounds
in our swollen limbs.

Shoes are old and broken;
Ammi welds them with rubber
and welded add-ons
add to weight.

Fear is all to feed on
and vegetables:
Shaftal[2], *Shoarki*[3] and *Thoasla*[4]
alone to extend our breath on —
death's clatter rings near tonight.

Baba's muscled feet
cut through the crispy snow,
tracing the footprints of moon
in the freezing fist of night

to smuggle rice
and fill the hollowed stomachs;
medications
to patch the aged wounds —
death's clatter rings near tonight.

Dahmardah, a compound of ghosts.
The Taliban's heinous anthem roars high —
they are here to break faith,
holding the funded swords
against the confined souls,
aggrieved as frozen leaves —
death's clatter rings near tonight
and gods are the commanders.

November 11, 2017
Cisarua, Bogor, Indonesia

—

In memory of
Shukria Tabassum (9)
Mohammad Sadiq (16) (cousin)
Mohammad Khan (28)
Shaukat Ali (13)
Chacha (nickname)
Lajaward (75)
Sar-daru
Abdul Hameed Yawari, 36 (brother-in-law)

—

1. *Karbala*: A city in central Iraq to the south of Baghdad; a holy city for Shiite Muslims. This is the site of the tomb to our beloved Prophet Mohammed's grandson who was martyred by a much larger force sent by Yazīd when prophet Mohammad's grandson stood against injustice and cruelty.
2. *Shaftal*: A local vegetable fed to the animals.
3. *Shoarki*: One of the home-grown vegetables that the locals collect in spring for consumption. Some dry them for winter use and some use them fresh.
4. *Thoasla*: A wild vegetable that grows in the mountains. It is one of many wild vegetables that the locals collect, cook and consume, either fresh or dried for later consumption.

Fragments of autumn leaf

The heat of colonisation
lays warm against my breast —
each sparkle, a needle,
crafting a shroud of red
from my velvet blood.

I see,
feel nothing but fire,
the plaintive smoke
dressed upon the crispy cheeks
of yellow evening,
    in the heat of dragons,
        risen from the depths of hell
        with decrees of genocide —
            carrying swords
        warmer than fire,
teeth sharper
than arrows of ruin —

swords against
the sweet summon of my *Hazaragi*[1] faith,
the reverend shade of my cheeks;
the artistic rhythms of my tongue
and the well-sown seeds
of my native roots.

        Baba and *Ammi* grown old,
                    burnt out
        shielding their chests;
        I burnt too
                facing the flames
                and melted to dust
                each time

Baba and *Ammi* gasped,
running onto mountains
or borders —
the end of the world

where they turned to August,
yellow leaves
befallen

from the amplitude of time
which cut the roots of all
that ever stood.

They gathered their bits,
stitched a shroud for each one of us
and placed our fragments
in the pouches,
made out of our skins
and ran.

We ran headlong
in wind's flamboyant waves
like sparrows with burned wings
as the festive fireworks,
hissed down our sky.

We ran afoot with no vision
from a shapeless dungeon of despair
with a few backpacks of wriggling memories,
memories of chopped off
arms of white,
bare in shirt-sleeves,
hanging out of burning windows.

We turned into pairs of ragged claws,
scrabbling on our scooped fingernails
and crawled on our stretched-out knees.

/...

As we ran,
Mustafa was running too;
he was running faster
than his failing feet shuffled
amid deafening screams —
screams that could shake the heart of God.

I couldn't bid a goodbye
or hug home's fallen walls
nor could *Ammi* drag
the browned bodies
out of the bleeding holes.

We ran
with smashed piles of feet
over the hard edges of rocks and thorns
and in the shades of burning breeze.

We ran against the scaling mountains,
dragging ourselves forward in the bushes
and beaten through the blades of wheat.

We ran
among the raging heat of bombs,
unable to pull the bodies out
to cover
or check their pulse
under their broken ribs.

Ammi held my hand tight and we ran.
Ammi with one shoe on;
one left behind.

She panted in the long smoke-tainted fields,
dense like those rockets,
jolting the trackless land
into a mound of powder.

A burning bullet
floated on *Ammi*'s shoulder
as we were heaving
in the open palms of faithless farmland.

Ammi fell, scattered —
	bits of autumn leaf,
I fell in the wild bushes,
stretched on my face —
a worn-out canvas.

Ammi attempted to run on,
fell back on her face,
she stood to run
but fell again.

I engulfed the flames,
stuck in my throat
trying to lift *Ammi* up,
she fell again
		and again
		as though the parched soil
		was pulling her down,
		thirsty for a drop of fresh gore.

With *Ammi*'s fingers inside the wound
	trying to stem the blood,
teetering over rubbles
with hills of hell,
swaying upon us.

We kept running with broken bones
until a few splendid hillsides
tenderly embraced to shield us
from the rushing bullets —
the raindrops of iron.

/...

The sky was a vast turbulence of flames,
pouring shards of steel —
arrows of metal
and the universe gathered
     for a heartless revenge —
a full conduct of final annihilation.

        The whizz of militants' weaponries
        and blows of flare in the air
        indicated the fall of lives;
        the urge to escape.

    We ran until we could no longer run,
    cried until we could no longer cry,
    until our vision could no longer hold
    the image of Dahmardah,
    sinking in storms of smoke.

We did not leave home by choice.
We escaped from carnage,
the smearing bullets,
loud like gods' applauding sound.

We ran with our fast-pumping hearts,
tightly wrapped in our palms,
the dead faces of young and old,
fragments of burning lungs
hid under our sleeves.

We did not leave home by choice.
We escaped the stalking death.
We sighed,
mourned,
sipped our boiling blood
each time gasping
for a last breath.

I was born to die.
Each time I died,
I was returned
to die again.

February 15, 2021
Bogor, Indonesia

---

1. *Hazaragi* (Noun): Refers to the Hazara people or their language.

Death lies far and wide
For my dearest brother, Abdul Ahad

Abdul Ahad and I
hide below fireflies,
in a long cave
under a tree of sweet apricot —
200 metres away from our castle.

This dark, dreary *Somoch*[1],
cave of ancients,
leads to an old well,
many years dry.

War has riven life,
death lies far and wide;
shootings are loud and close,
landing rockets shake the cave,
wrapping up our moans.

Dust falls on our unowned skulls
as if the world is falling apart —
each sand a bullet,
cutting through my skin.

Seconds surpass months;
hours wear the veil of years;
darkness buried us alive —
no blood left to run in veins,
legs are numb
unable to sit or lay,
faces too sensitive
unable to cry.

Terror gusts in;
we resemble coal miners
with traces of wrinkled lines,
left on our frozen cheeks.

I hear one familiar voice —
Ammi's.
She comes once in the morning,
once in the evening
to extend our breath.

A speeding arrow of metal
cut through Abdul Ahad's right foot —
in between his middle toes,
red liquid covers the ground,
blowing fragrance of raw meat.

It has reached his delicate limbs,
eyes overly exhausted to weep,
lungs have swollen,
too fragile to beat.

We are abandoned here
to remain alive —
only flies swarm around
to offer us company.

He shrivels up,
barely groans,
weakly raising his hands
across his face
to ease the annoyance.
Brother in a distant fog.

I try to cover his body;
hide his injured foot with a *satranji*[2]
but the flies keep chanting,
sucking the leaking blood
from above the bandage.

Once in a while,
he stares through deep-set eyes,

/...

pleading for my presence,
a guardian
as he lays here
    like a paralysed soldier,
      left behind
      in the venomous shadows of war.

    Grief invades my visions
and I gaze in long pauses,
wishing I could take
some of his agony away
as his fainting lament
makes its way to my barren chest —
mournful and cold.

January 22, 2019
Jakarta, Indonesia

—

1. *Somoch*: Cave
2. *Satranji*: Rug

Ruins of war

Visions unlocked,
>wept over my childhood spring,
>ruined by the dark cloud of war.

I moved my lips to form the word home,
but flood of blood rushed down
>over my cradle,
>rocks and sands
>filled my mouth.

>I stood muted,
>blank,
>cold
>and torn off
>of earth and sky;
>>died before I was fully formed,
>>>before I learned how to smile.

>>>I died with each breath
>>>that begged to remain alive
>>>and returned to life
>>>>with my lungs,
>>>>pouring out
>>>>of my mouth.

>>The signs of life
>>were struck off within me
>>in so many ways;
>my tongue has lost its rhymes.

I've gone numb,
numb as my words;
dead as rocks.

/...

I don't regard death as a rival
but a fine friend,
giving a hand
to pull these arrows
from my plaintive bosom
and guide me home.

August 17, 2018
Cisarua, Bogor, Indonesia

The nine troubled tombs
One poem in segments

Segment one

Homes to complete ruins,
highlands
robbed,
stolen;

farms,
bare,
bruised.

Cultural rituals,
confiscated,
banned.

Every ten miles
lays a massive graveyard —
mysteries of forlorn souls,
flesh extracted,
melted on roasted torsos.

A few tarry trees
alone to stare back;

the remains of skeletons
with arrow-holes on shoulders,
guarding their forefathers' castles —

the glorified legends
with ritual names,
frozen upon the edges
of unclean tongues.

But I'm not afraid
to recall their names,

/...

nor shall be misled
by the lies of the censors.

I recollect their stolen smiles,
reinstate their shattered images;
restore their erased imaginations,
recompose their hijacked strength
to form them whole.

You can't prohibit their visions,
their weathered beams and spirits
with the dust of years,
or bury them under your grimy turbans.

Now that
the wind of time blows fair,
together
we shall put them on full display
and exhibit the secrets,
the turbaned brutes in their war clubs
fear the world to see.

Come and be the witness
for me to recite the lyrics
of those long-forgotten tombs
whose songs you wish to hear.

Hold my hands
to uplift the lanterns of justice
and sow them on those sacred lands,
trophied to the paid troops of winds,
armed by the torrent of storms
to uproot the ancient seeds
willingly and with pleasure.

Segment two

Qandahar,
home to broken fingers,
stock of human trade
where the enslaved Hazaras
were swapped with camels.

> Jalalabad,
> the current embodiment
> of false ownership,
> overrun by branded goats.

Shari Safa,
the unknown tomb to many wombs
where the nightingales mourn
in Hazaragi dialects at noon;
weep over the unsaid silence
at nights with moon.

> Janda,
> where our footprints guide
> into a thousand gardens of tulips —
> emergent trays of jewels,
> arisen from the cheeks of heaven.

Moqoor,
the exiled spring of Hazaragi breath
where the butterflies burn their wings
over every wound when autumn arrives.

> Gilan,
> the worn-out orchard of forgotten graves
> where Hazaragi blood runs deep
> and mountains pour forward
> the eternal streams of aged grief.

/...

Bakhtu,
where babies were lulled to sleep in Dahmardah
to the brave cadence
of Ghulam Haidar Khan's breath
and his courageous companions.

Ghazni,
the ritual land of festivity
where the Hazaragi accent chants
in ancient rhymes —
the glad summon of Azan,
a consolation,
enlivens the aggrieved hearts.

Parwan,
where Qala-e-Hazara stands strong
like the realms of *Salsal*[1] and *Shahmama*[2].

———

1. *Salsal*: The larger statue of Buddha in Bamiyan, traditionally identified
   as a male figure.
2. *Shahmama*: Queen Mother. The smaller statue of Buddha in Bamiyan,
   identified as a female figure.

Segment three

And I'm here,
splintered,
burdened,
bruised
with lungs scattered
into the wide fields of nonexistence.

Sometimes in doomed alleyways,
sometimes within the fist of
a cold and silent room.

My lungs thrown toward the godless sky,
feeding a kind of human,
more ravenous than wolves.

Yet, when I behold
the charming beauty of my homeland,
my bits re-join each other;
heart beats to life,
the chest filled
with the yearning fire
slows down,
my pen reloads letters,
building a bridge
between my soul
and those arid deserts,
I once called home.

Those are my lands,
the lands of all Hazaras.

The arid spaces are surely mine,
the swift clouds too.

Every wind whispers my name,
every star portrays my identity;
every rock mirrors my face.

/...

I hear them breathing
Baba's soulful songs of stars
through each banana leaf at Puncak.

Chest forward,
I repeat the anthem —
every thread of breath beats for life
and I am clothed
by the homing garment of snow,
silently twinkling under a full moon —

a thousand rays of light,
there are, to be worshipped

and I ask each one,
are you still mine?

October 28, 2021
Pajajaran Bogor Indonesia

72

Kohl of ashes

There is a place
      where every child knows
      the word gun before pen,
          war before peace —

a place
          where every child knows
             the word *Infijar*[1]
                before a rockstar —
      kill before heal,
      Tab-eaz[2] before *Tarkhis*[3]

There is a place
      where every child knows
      the word flee before free,
      refugee before nationality —
          violence before silence;
               migration before imagination —

a place
      where every child knows
      the word detention-centre
      before learning-centre;
      labour before leader.

There is a place
    where every child knows
      the word persecutor before protector;
      Pakistan before Afghanistan,
        Iran before Laghman,
          Baluchistan before Kandahar,
            Islamabad before Jalalabad
            Qom before Kabul,
               Sydney before Saighan,
                 Germany before Taimani

/...

Turkey before Taloqan,
Belgium before Bamiyan,
Cisarua before Charikar.

There is a place
where the dawn asks permission
from goats to break;
Mullahs[6] bribe God with popcorn
to manipulate their speech —
a place
where the radicals sue education,
hiding behind the veils of *ustads*[4]
scared that the ink of reality
burn holes in their *shalwar*[5].

There is a place
where *Mullahs* and politicians
employ their daughters to dress in dollars
but teach others to dress in
the rotten skins of potatoes —

a place,
where singing poetry is *Haram*[7],
Quran *Halal*[8];
grief joy;
joy grief —

a place
where I smelt blood
at every riverbank,
I collected water from;
saw red flesh on tree branches
more than the green leaves.

There is a place
>where the radicals oil their hair
>from ponds of human blood,
>put kohl in their eyes
>with the ashes of Hazaragi shroud.

December 06, 2016
Cisarua, Bogor, Indonesia

---

1. *Infijar*: Explosion.
2. *Tab-eaz*: Discrimination.
3. *Tarkhis*: When one completes a compulsory military service and gets discharged.
4. *Ustads*: Masters.
5. *Shalwar*: Pants.
6. *Mullahs*: Religious scholars.
7. *Harum*: Forbidden by Islamic law.
8 *Halal*: Allowed by Islamic law.

Racer of death

Shadow of genocide
sat upon me
like the spiral storm —

stalking me

at late sundown
and in the sun's rebirth at dawn —

in towns and villages,
ruined at their core —

in unknown tombs like *Kandi Pusht*[1],
where the rented pigs with darted beards,
nailed me in a live shooting line
alongside my tribesmen,
where the valley of death
stared right into my eyes,
hungry for *Hazaragi* flesh,
where wafts of rotten skins,
oily bones filled the air
with the smell of fermented fish.

At dark seas,
where youthful Hazaras
became a tender meal
to starving sharks.

The traces of death I ran in,
are countless,
valleys I cried with,
drowned in my blood;
clouds I sought refuge of,
left me alone and homeless.

Deserts are my middle name,
borderlands the other half —
in the journeys
to deserts,
valleys
and borders,
I was taken as a hostage,
put in the marketplace
and sold off
like the son of *Payambar*[2] Yaqub,
Hazrat[3] *Yusuf*.

Each one bought,
blindfolded with my own skin,
chained me with the threads,
excision of my heart.

I have been lifted up high
then routinely grounded,
but I gathered myself up —
ran frightened,
facing oblivion in confusion,
hiding my wrinkled scars
to pursue a healing in mankind.

But each one I ran to,
poured in my scars
a handful of hot chilli;
rubbed salt instead of
shrouding with a bandage.

Each one I ran to,
dumped me in incarcerating camp,
where I was squeezed
between their reddish fists
until I vomited
every sip of my mother's milk.

/...

The cruelty in mankind,
an acid that burned me off
and I melted to ashes
bit
by
bit
with no breath
to be gasped;
no sound
to be sighed.

I live with the intimate heartache,
burning beneath my skin;
the reefs of traumas
that heave upon my chin.

They shake and I scream.
They roar and I die within.

December 26, 2015
Cisarua, Bogor, Indonesia

———

1. *Kandi Pusht*: In the 1990s the Hazara people were selectively taken off
   vehicles there and arrogantly shot.
2. *Payambar*: Messenger of God.
3. *Hazrat*: An Arabic word, used to show: presence, dignity, Majesty, Highness,
   Excellency and Holiness.

Swallow scent from scars

of tyre-necklaces,
rigid and tight
　　　　around *Hazaragi* necks,

　　burnt-out skulls
　　with eyeballs,

　　hanging
　　　　　　　upon

　　　　　　　fractured　　　chests,

　　exploded tongues,
　　scorched between tarnished lips
　　in smoke-filled streets.

Blood-curdling for mothers,
prisoners of misfortune,
a sightless death-trench
to babies under the rage
of 'ringing stars' —

or the blossoms of school roses,
quailing at the stench of blood;
sore soil twisted against the tides,
except the multitude of red flood —
　　　　streams of rose colour

　　invisible graveyards,
　　piles of native heads —

　　a battle ground to gruesome wars
　　where tyrants steal colour from tulips
　　and swallow scent from the scars.

May 19, 2011
Puli Surkh, Kart-e-3, Kabul, Afghanistan
(From the warm embrace of mother)

Wails of hidden horror

Paired missiles explode
like the hurried eruptions of volcanoes —
a brutish proclamation of death
over life.

Barren homes, blown-up walls,
limbs twist like infernal bodies,
screams echo
as fast slicing swords strike
off every onyx-eyed gaze.

Heart beats in long pauses
as drones of bullets dive around —
each one forges in,
carries spells of death.

Townlets are lonely cemeteries;
terrors cannot veil themselves anymore —
they eat from inside out
like termites at an eternal feast.

      Each event lives under my skin
      like haunting creatures,
      concealed in dark tunnels.

Quiet places with less crowd
are scary,
unmanageable,
      death squeezes
      into a tight hug
      from all corners.

Faces,
conversations, sounds and smells
stir up memories
into episodes of nightmares —
real as I re-live.

Fireworks are fascinating
but harsh cries of death,
reminder of rotating rockets;
blasting roars of missiles
or sunken groans for help
from beneath the realms of debris,

A wall of hidden fear sets forth,
dragging me into a sunless world
and ties me to sharp strings of life.

Of all that ended,
contains fresh images of living beasts,
the leftover of pungent darkness
to live with.

Only survivors of wars
can feel the weight of loss
and a bleeding soldier,
abandoned
in the heat of a battlefield.

June 23, 2017
Bogor, Indonesia

IV

ABANDONED IN THE HEAT /
CAPTIVE OF THE HILLS /
FISH IN A DESERT /
BIRD IN THE FROST

متروك در گرما \ اسیر تپه ها \

ماهی در کویر \ پرنده در سرما \

"Abandoned in The Heat, Captive of The Hills,
Fish in a Desert, Bird in The Frost" is a Persian
poem I grew up hearing from my father.

Whose tongue has swollen in Abdul's ruins?

The glorious morning breaches darkness;
Ammi sets *Subhana*[1] on the orb
of a wide colourful *Sufra*[2] —
red and light grey.

     Clay pot of steaming tea
     on earthen red *Patnoos*[3]
     and the cheerful beams of sunrise
     greet us with warmth.

White salty cheese,
fragrant bank of mint
wakes every sense of appetite up —
each fluffy leaf is carefully rested
upon the breast of a brown plate
with a few slices of organic butter
            next to be embraced
            by freshly baked *Naan*[4].

     I lean on *Madar Kalan*'s shoulders,
     gazing at an old Panasonic TV screen,
     running a sad entertaining show:
            pleading voices of mothers,
            husky cries of numb children,
            formless frames of fathers,
    dangle of quivering heads,
curly and wrinkled flesh,
stretched out upon the bony chins.

                                /...

Them in thin clothes
scars can be spotted through,
shoes tattered;
faces worn out
pale as our cracked clay pot;

'starving babies' —
piles of bones
with sunken bellies
on their ossified backs,
sinking in the spars of fog,
in the salty sniff of sea broth.

They heave ahead into the sedgy grass
and gulping fields by the seashore
with no purpose.

Weeping mothers stuck in mud,
teenagers run,
they crumble,
chasing the deathly tracks.

A mother carries her inflamed baby —
lips dry and parched,
fractured as fragments
of our bombed-out cups.

She grabs her baby like a mother-cat,
runs toward the leaping sea —
one hand locked on her bag,
the other loses her baby
in a quick swarm of flood.

All fall on the ground
like shattered beads of pearls;
the mother too
as her shuffling feet fail
to handle the striking sticks.

She barely stands on her dazed feet;
falls on her face,
crawling in the water
like a wounded fish.

What are they doing, Madar Kalan?
Running for their lives, son.

Too young to fathom this war-worn movie
but can feel the burden
as fear builds up.

I shrink behind *Madar Kalan*,
covering my eyes beneath her *Chadar*[5],
not knowing that one day
I will run faster than them;
Ammi will cry harder
in between the interior gravity of war
and I will be aired on a TV screen —
all eyes leaping on me.

Yes,
it is me today,
framed inside the tube:
Abdul Samad Haidari.

/...

Abdul
who escapes into dark seas
in full submission to death;
becomes a meal poet
to the mineral sharks
with inability
to cry anything
              but blood.

Abdul
who hides in seas,
seeking a mending
from the castles of salt.

Abdul
who stands naked
of all human identity,
stripped of
              all belonging
by earth's ironic hands.

Abdul
who belongs nowhere —
not even a piece of shroud
dares to enclose
his bewildered eyes.

The forgotten *Abdul*
who groans like a lonely camel
through the tangled reefs of jungles —
with no beginning or end.

Abdul
who is lost in winding roads
with barefoot-heart,
biting the leftovers of his lungs
behind the moist walls of camps.

Abdul
who has fallen off
his mother's embrace,
became red drops of rain,
pouring in alleyways,
fully anonymous.

No one ever crosses these alleyways
but the obscure silence,
or midnight katydids,
screaming with him
over the corpses of his dreams,
crucified
in a thousand rifts of time.

Abdul
on whom they banned the sky
from pouring the craving warmth of life
until his heart ran out of light;
eyes turned into seas of silence.

Abdul
who became a death seeker —
and yet
of all deaths

/...

whose hands freeze,

voice shivers

when they approach him.

January 11, 2021
Bogor, Indonesia

———

1. *Subhana*: Breakfast.
2. *Sufra*: Table cloth, spread on the floor on which dishes of food are placed for a meal.
3. *Patnoos*: Tray.
4. *Naan*: A flat, leavened bread, made of wheat flour and baked in the tandoor.
5. *Chadar*: A large piece of cloth that covers the head and upper body of females — especially worn by Muslim women.

Home rides in backpack

I carry my home in a small backpack.
This is my pillow on homing footpaths,
a blanket on cold, moist sidewalks.

Its straps keep me calm
Its hug wraps me warm.

In it, I snail.

In it I bury shards of young memories,
memories of joy and grief;
stained pieces of my broken pen
and the burnt pages of my school books.

On it are etched *Baba*'s fingerprints,
Ammi's hurried desperate teardrops
and Hakima's last swollen gazes.

In it I carry the bombed soil of my hometown,
the silent woes of my crumbled walls,
the aromatic mists of my mud-made house
and the lush wetlands of our withered lives.

It reminds me of *Baba*'s last helpless look,
sisters' boiling rushing teardrops,
brothers' final fearful hugs
and *Ammi*'s last worried embrace.

With it I ran across the jungle,
climbed the piercing wire-fenced borders;
sailed upon the sad sweeps of lost waves.

With it I became a mist,
glued on mango leaves.

/...

89

With it I shared my lonely anguish
when the hermit walls of camp
banned my existence.

In it resides every bit of me,
the worn-out adulthood remembrance,
the inward sorrows
and the stifled groans.

Together,
we survived cruel caves of the underworld.
It measures the length of time,
the hosts detained their guests.

In it are debased surprises,
the uncontained sighs
and the midnight muffled cries.

In it are debarred the old-time songs,
springing in my soul,
cold and distress;
the unfolded lyrics,
paused upon my stolen tongue.

In it I bury layers of yearning
under arrest,
the past-tracing hymns,
stuck in my veins.

In it are living
the rest of me that is banned,
the sighed sounds of baffled lands
and the sea-groans at shorelines
where God denied to hold my hands.

But it has been awhile now,
my muscled arms begin to weaken;

I run out of that childish stamina,
    unable to carry it further.

My vision glazes over,
    too weak to hold that old-time sight.
I'm falling lower than my hopes —
    tiny ribs, skulls,
hip bones —
all moan in pain
and my sky seems exhausted,
weeping with no rain.

But when this bruised heart
    bids the last goodbye,
these stubborn eyes shut,
    close forever,
bury my backpack alongside me
    or place it under my bewildered head —

so I, who forgot my childhood songs,
    get reborn in the bosom of stars
and recompose this poem,
    I wrote in days of oppression
so it can be recited aloud and free.

October 23, 2017
Cisarua, Bogor, Indonesia

Wrath of the sea

Flakes of shadows unfold,
    curling over
    like mountains of tar,
    stealing every sparkle from eyes
    that searches for life.

      As I flood on board,
      the leaping waves whirl inward,
blowing rumours of death
to the worn-out wooden boat
that keeps chasing a split moon.

      Wind, the arrow flames,
      burning me to ashes;
      sour water dives deep
      within the scars
      and the burns keep me alive.

When the starving sharks shake our boat,
loud screams of wingless butterflies
remind me of the grief of Noah (AS)[1] —
He wept over his drowning valleys;
we, over our swollen home
and a doomed destination

      with no light or stars
      but hateful slogans
      that shoot the heat
      of double standards
      against our worn-out chests;

we collide against the same beclouded world
wherever the yields of the sea push us.

When shall this caravan reach
the realm of no loneliness?

Uncounted
Unlabelled
Visible
Free.

July 29, 2014
Malaysian Sea, a border line between two worlds.

---

1. (AS): *Alayhis salaam* (Peace be upon him).

Tell borders to be kinder

It's midnight at the shoreline;
heart sinks in hard sands,
feet have no place to land.

> Darkness bribes the rain
> to shut me down,
> ears are hearkened
> to exploding sounds of thunder
> that shakes the chest
> of unrelenting ground.

Exhausted legs hang
off my skinny frame,
unable to drag them on —
thick fog covers my eyes
as though I am swimming
in pools of tar —
not knowing
which one to jump in first.

No helping hand to borrow,
except the thorny bars
> of jungle to wade through,
> seeping through the fresh wounds
> on my right thigh.

> Drowsy faces of children,
> the torn maps,
> > guiding ahead,

> scared mothers' isolated groans,
> the fading signals to chase fate.

Striving fathers stride ahead
like thick, shrouded hazes —

hair caked with salty mud,
smelling of consuming death —
lost in the human-brought tragedy.

> Torn sacks on their extended backs,
> ensigns of horror, old photographs,
> rotting memories of friends, families —
> daughters' fearful gazes
> and sons' stolen sighs.

> > They gather all their pieces,
> > crumble onward
> > into unseen fragments
> > of dark clouds for shelter
> > but sink low in the flood.

> Visions lose the hold of earth
> and chests crush against
> > the towered tides of dark water
> > that prevent their quick escape.

Some make it to a hard wooden boat,
floating like plastic bottles;
some vanish in the depth of sea,
becoming a quick meal —
another tragic memory.

I drown and die too
until the taste of salt revives
and the flute of cold wind penetrates.

All swallow sorrows in,
shivering in fear and hunger
as their mournful mouths
slowly whisper prayers
for a safer place to hide.

/...

I, too, pray and weep,
holding tight my memories
inside my wet postbag,
tucked against
my panting heart.

O God,
tell borders to be kinder.

July 27, 2014
Malaysian Shoreline

The lavish night

I dwell,
        drown in taut tides
        of the underworld shadows
        with no sign of light and love.

Sky squeezes
        from above,
the scorching earth
        from beneath;
borders of barbed-wire fences
        from front;
iron bars of camps
        from behind.

The heat of colonial gods
turned me blind —
eyes behold no colour,
face has lost its glow.

        This fractured skull
        no longer belongs to me,
        nor have thoughts the oxygen
        for expression,

    visions are caged birds —
    no space to shake
    or spread their wings.

I stand in the red mouth of hell
naked of all rights;
lost in between
the pages of thick valleys.

        I greet myself
        with the dust of time

/...

from the broken jars of
my own phrase-less words
in thousand sighs,
to balance in my arrested soul
with the left-overs of a past

        that sticks in my head
        like the lavish nights of war
with a funeral of trauma,
pressed against my soul.

I sob and swallow
my own lungs up,
      pained and bruised —

    skin torn from flesh,
    flesh removed from bones.

I'm a bowl of raw meat
on the tables of the wicked.

January 04, 2017
Cisarua, Bogor, Indonesia

Swords of tyranny

Teaching the walls how to weep

Walk in these dark-interior walls,
follow the overriding echoes of groans
and I will guide you
to the heat-struck roses,
captives with stolen colour;
dumped in the crushing reefs
of inflaming camps

                    red
                    smoky
                    oily;

                              away from camera lenses —
                              sad, silenced
                              alone, anguished —

                    dumped piles of bones,
                    barren and bruised,
                    shattered and gored
                    stained the walls.

A place,
sour and silent
silent and scary
scary and isolated.

                    A place,
                    where the moon is under arrest,
                    it boils to the surface with fear;
                    stars are prisoners,
                    hiding from the guarding hyenas,

                    disguised in uniforms of charm,
                    feeding on flesh of children,

                                                  /...

caste aside on purple crossroads
with lips apart,
shells, empty of life,
grieving with grey evenings.

A place,
crowded yet empty
as fainted gazes
except the moulding woes
of labelled guests
whose existence is forbidden,
marks no rank than death itself,
aspires nothing
but their disjointed cheeks —

        each surging droplet
           a thousand beads of dreams
           and grief unheard
              rushing

                 down,

                        down

        making a hundred prostrations
        on the solid breast of rough roadways —
        fractionated drops of their beings,
        their unowned hopes,
        drizzling low on asphalts
        trembled under the feet of vague mobs.

Somewhere
isolated from earth and space
where rivers are running
by two round fountains
and the fire in their breasts
roar like a camel in rage.

Somewhere
life stops like a period,
air doesn't exist to breathe —
> impervious not to pity;
> jasmine blossoms
> are the colour of faces;
> clouds are red
> and walls,
>> the dark webs
>> of indefinite prisons,
>> unable to find
>> or measure itself.

> Somewhere
> they have extracted scent
> and colour from human skin —
> oceans are *Sharbat*[1] of red;
> streets, faithless
> as of the bribed courts.

Somewhere
my pained soul is scripted
into every line and verse —
rhymes crafted out of rigid threads
with chains of iron round my wrist
and swords of tyranny on my tongue.

Somewhere,
Annihilation
Depression
Oppression
Suicidal thoughts
echo through the chambers of barbarism

>> but the figure sinks in vain;
>> wiped out from diary of recollections
>> with heavy hands,

/...

choking up the golden lights
in favour of double standards.

Here human love didn't arrive
but certainly, the pretended one,
harming
destroying,
terrorising.

Psychiatrists instill PTSD
Specialists teach
how to die.

December 17, 2018
Cisarua, Bogor, Indonesia

---

1. *Sharbat*: A sweet drink, prepared from fruits or flower petals.

Where is the way out?

I drift along,
looking for stars,
lost in dark sunless paths
with no sense of a beginning
nor an end.

I can't figure things out
in this long curvy road,
nor can I see a light ahead
except the looming shadows
of colonisation and atrocity
where everyone is active,
digging holes under the banana trees
to wrap the slain bodies in
so no trace be found.

My heart grows heavy and sore,
lungs white and thin —
no common air
dares to run through,
no blood left to flow.

Help me
erase these tattoos
from my forehead;
numbers off my cheeks.

Give me a hand,
unchain my feet
and set me free.

March 29, 2016
Cisarua, Bogor, Indonesia

On the pavement tonight

The narrow sky grows drowsy,
sun sinks, pink-coloured;
brightness declines to stay
over the part-blue broken tent.

I draw aside to write,
my hand trembles
as I feed the vanquishing parchment
with the rose-coloured toner,
linked straight to my heart-cells.

A few limping sparrows lay afront
with fading eyes
fixed upon the bystanders
who hold arrows with pleasure,
aiming between your eyebrows
while whispering in pitiless dialects
rumours of cold.

It's bitter when I inhale
and burns the pavement,
my chest, I mean.

Ghazni sparrows wander around —
some dozed off on the burning paths
out of hunger and traumas,
some shake under plastic tents,
struck by words
sharper than blades.

Young sparrows' dusty foreheads and cheeks,
tattered mattress on camels' backs —
wrinkled skins of wooden coffins.

My thoughts solidify,
become whole, reasoned;
steeped in, soaked up,
absorbed by the family's condition.

Feelings clash together like sea tides,
thoughts twist into stormy thunders;
I swallow hard to hold them hidden,
to mask the growing empathy
that will spin me out of control.

The noise of *ojeks*[1] and cars
on the road distract me;
orang-orang pulang kerja[2]
pass by with shiny shoes,
blue masks covering their faces.

They later look like surgeons on the street,
hunting for *bakso*[3] or *nasi goreng*,[4]
surgeons, just out of their operating theatres,
fragile moods hanging in inquisitive eyes.

The refugee-homed pavement

Now,
the crowded pavement drones
with distressed sparrows,
dust covers their faces —

/...

they look like bedraggled war-torn returnees,
lips parched and cracked
as Afghanistan's bombed out streets.

Their eyes are round-sunken
like tops of arid,
                    deserted wells.

When they stare back,
their pleading eyes appear to be
                              the broken headlights on cars,
                              abandoned long ago.

The children
Ghazni baby sparrows
persistently ask for the ice-creams,
they see melting upon local students' lips,
returning home from school in decent uniforms.

The Father
The father sparrow anxiously rubs his wings;
his eyes float, barely open,
defying gravity, aggrieved —
those eyes contemplate
the passing crowd in distance,
helplessly wondering
if anyone would fill their lantern
to burn tonight.

The Mother

> She sits in uttermost silence,
> numbed,
> eyes fixed upon her husband
>   in   extended   gaps,
> gulping her brinish tears.

>   She does not utter a word,
>   just stares at the man,
>   she once knew well
> who is now left cast aside
> with his young Afghani dignity,
> trampled like a priceless treasure
> under the feet of Wrongs.

The family

them with nothing to eat,
them with everything to fear —
gasping dust from shuffling shoes
and roadside exhaust fumes.

> Hunger does not harden,
> like trauma and disappointment do.

> Will death turn its back on them again
> or stalk when earth wears the veils of dark?

> Will Afghani blood drench the ground
> or flow across The Styx?

/...

Fat heads pop out from windows once in a while
but extend no hands of mercy —
not even those in coloured uniforms.

These people are left alone
under the heat of colonial gods
who eat children and abandon the remains
in the dimming fist of empty night.

December 14, 2017
Kalideres, Jakarta, Indonesia

To all my fellow refugees who are still in Kalideres.
My heart bleeds each time the images of your pale faces
and parched lips fly before my eyes.

———

1. *Ojeks*: Motorcycle taxis.
2. *orang-orang pulang kerja*: People going home after work.
3. *Bakso*: Or *baso*. An Indonesian meatball, or meat paste, made from beef surimi. Its texture is similar to the Chinese beef ball, fish ball, or pork ball. The word bakso refers to a single meatball or the complete dish of meatball soup.
4. *Nasi goreng*: An Indonesian fried rice dish, usually cooked with pieces of meat and vegetables.

The red glares

Here
       I
              am
far
                     out
        tangled

in a labyrinth of mysteries,
twists and turns,
with no name or address
where mosses are barbed-wires,
burying the trace of agony.

                    Here the sun seeks approval to rise
                    unlike the choking fog,
                    swinging through the motionless
                    shoulders of mountains
                    with limbs embrace,
         scattering ashes of human bones
         with dry droplets of blood
         upon the jumbled
         piles of sweating rocks.

Here fences are made out of human arms,
rooves are covered by human skin
and our groans are dry thunders
without a dewdrop of rain.

Here the oiled-city
is a rough court of injustice
and the ground is a molten carpet —
one can neither stand
nor lay or sit.

                                    /...

No solitude in the human forest
or enough room for human love
in their mossy hearts
but red glares
upon the burnt holes.

December 23, 2018
Cisarua, Bogor, Indonesia

Abandoned here, driven from there

I'm fine but
pained and perishing,
shaking, shouted and shrinking,
excluded and betrayed,
trapped, terrified and tortured,
downed, drowned and full of dread.

I'm fine but
detained, controlled and uprooted,
bruised, blamed and bullied,
terrorised, victimised and abandoned,
sad, separated and enslaved,
denied and devalued.

I'm fine but
misplaced, misunderstood and misused,
silenced, scared and suspended,
wronged, reduced and ripped off.

I'm fine but
deprived, dull and dying,
numb, nervous and neglected,
alone, lifeless and longing,
cold and crushed.

I'm fine but
with no tongue to speak,
the butchers sliced it off

with bamboo blade
on a metal table
at the left corner of camp —

ready to chop
my head off

/...

if one more word
breaches the canvas.

    Predators too,
    feasted their eyes —
    through the cracked walls
    on the other side of
    the blood dripping sea.

Their fangs, sword of Yazid;
eyes sharper than laser,
burning a thousand holes
in my chest.

August 14, 2014
Cisarua, Bogor, Indonesia

Surrounded by the mourning frogs

Coldness and solitude host the night;
the distant *kampung*[1] hushed,
power is off like the hope in my eyes —
only a few rays of the dim moon
seep through the wooden window slats.

I follow their drifting pathway,
looking up at the snoring sky
with its hazy eyes
slightly open —
God's face is veiled in intimate thought.

Two hours later

It runs as dark as my life,
dim as thick fog.
Rain pours;
packed jungle enfolds,
wrapping me in its moist arms.

Sounds break in the sky,
groaning sighs
amidst the flashing strikes
and every nerve cries.

I'm sore bone to bone
as I bed on this humid floor —
Hell is here and I burn in its flame.

Four hours later

God drizzles slowly, seems tired
must be running out of tears;
frogs anguish,
they mourn;

/...

their croaks compose in cacophony,
a dirge for me —
They sing songs of grey in my heart.

Tempo of these amphibian voices slows down,
their pitch deepens
as light morning dawn approaches,
breaching the night's inhospitable hold.

Now,
bright hope floods over the ghostly *kampung*;
the terrifying frogs turn friendly too,
singing warm songs of new beginnings
in the honour of dawn.

Me,
now vertical,
singing in my heart
the songs of resurrection
and triumph.

I survived the night
but not the solitude.

August 09, 2017
Cisarua, Bogor, Indonesia

—

1. *Kampung*: Means village in Bahasa Indonesia.

Games of double standards

War breaks,
bullets, missiles dive in —
a thousand cries of anguish,

your eyes meet the flame;
heart feels the burden of death.

    You run curve
    in circle,
    round,
    fall down,
    scramble up;

    run again,
    looking at
    no direction;
    no purpose.

    Darkness,
    a hole in a rock
    to hide,
    to take refuge.

You don't look for a window,
neither a door —
no one holds your hands
and pulls you out
but yourself alone.

There is no
East
West
North
South.

No destination,
destination chooses you —

                            /...

a sheep for meat,
blindfolded,
sold hand to hand.

Aiding dictators in two masks
with swords of double standards
on your throat,
chains of slavery
around your feet —
    slobber-mouths
    athirst for milk
    to sip;
    tears
    to sell.

The golden hair,
green eyes
fair skin —
bear higher demands.

Browns and blacks
are like TV screens
    on = alive
    off = dead
by a remote
in the red hands of dictators.

Their moods switch
when to turn on
or shut off.

Otherwise,
abandoned screens of black,
buried under the dust of time.

June 08, 2015
Cisarua 6:54am, Bogor, Indonesia

At his send-off

An epitaph for a refugee who was murdered in Indonesia.

Evening is cold and crawling
with a few paled refugees,
sitting around his lifeless face
under the weight of undreamt sky,

sore and silent,
silence that cuts through you
and wraps life up.

Fear and grief
shrouded their desperate eyes —
oblivious to pain:
numb to life
like wilted leaves in autumn
with nothing left to cling to.

A few numbed teardrops
alone to chase the silence away
as we enclose his muscled breast
in a worn borrowed shroud
ready to shoulder him
to his final home —

a kind of home,
where he rests enough
not to die
over
and over.

Locals, bystanders
are across this narrow lane,
no one comes forward
to share in his coffin
as good Muslims do,

/...

nor do they offer a word
at his last send off.

They stare at his passing funeral
like owls at noon;
some are whispering —
>   each stare,
>   a sword,
>   rumours, bullets,
>   burning a thousand cuts.

We carry him somewhere
unfamiliar to our feet,
so, we keep our eyes low
and move on deadly
under a yellow night
>   while fearfully moving our lips
>   to prayers
>   *La Illaha Illallah*[1]

>   Sods weep over his youthful body
>   as the shovel's blade
>   turns them upside down;
>   cold rocks shake in anguish
>   as we place his dreaming head over.

>   Only the moon's milky beams,
>   a dimmed lantern light
>   dares to accompany us —

creating a congregation
of sorrowful shadows
in our desolate mourning —

>   gazes of mourning only,
>   scared to utter aloud

because trees' ears can overhear,
thorny bushes have eyes —
                    these eyes may turn to words;
                    words may become arrows.

Looks communicate loud cries:
Who would send us off?
Who would be there
to close our eyes?

His narrow bed is hollowed
cold bricks, his pillow.
No tombstone to etch his name on
or epitaph to describe
who has stolen his life.

August 10, 2020
Jakarta, Indonesia

———

1. *La Illaha Illallah*: 'Nothing worshipped is worthy of worship except Allah'
   or 'There is no god truly worthy of worship except Allah.'

Between sea and fire

are containers of humans
caged migrating birds,

praying for safety

in realms of mountains
                    are tired souls
                    poured in

                    in tired places;

                    in whirlpools of sharks

                    and dead mountains

        shackled feet,

                abandoned
                on borderlands;

                piles of bones,
                deserted in blood-soaked camps

                red,
                cold —

        in seas,

                sour,

                swollen.

They are meant to be forgotten,
forced to endure death
with salted sands,
crammed between their cracked lips,
lungs, exploded out of sunken chests —

they have them all counted
and I saw your stares
burned holes in their cheeks.

The birds
you buried in your backyards
or pushed in swollen wombs of seas
had names on their foreheads
and those epitaphs
turned into universal anthems.

Echoes will keep ringing
in your sullen ears
for the years to come

and their names
shall bloom on your tongues
and swarms of butterflies
shall fill your mouth —

unable to be swallowed
or ejected.

January 13, 2017
Cisarua, Bogor, Indonesia

V
WE ARE ALIVE /
FOR THERE IS NO SHROUD

ما از بے کفنی زنده ایم

(The Green Offshore)

The original Persian proverb "Ma az bi kafani zindaim" translates as, "We are Alive for There is no Shroud." This proverb highlights the insight that the misfortunes and miseries in society are not caused by the absence of humans but rather the wickedness of certain individuals.

Diluted sharbat

Shadows of wicked camps,
cling in caves of nuclear cells;
we turn into powders
before the bare view of monsters,
forcing to breathe ourselves out.
Show us a way to the light
and guide us home.

They turned our past back to us
until we gave up on tomorrows;
puzzled us with lies
until we ran out of questions.
Chop these chains off our past
and guide us home.

We had enough of this world
but unrecognised,
gains, unpaid,
gains of our ruptured hearts
where we lulled ourselves to poems.
Break these metal cubes
and guide us home.

They offset our souls
painted shadows on the walls
are reflections of our fragmented dreams,
hidden from our own eyes.
Slice our tender flesh with mercy
or guide us home.

Loud promises
yet dark and cold,
echoing cunning burbles
in the desperate
night of autumn forest.

/...

O stars of heaven
lend us your visions
and guide us home.

They drink in our skulls
our diluted *Sharbat* (blood),
darkness silently overpowers
the light in our eyes;
      our veins have clotted,
      bones frigid,
life, a clean loss,
a barren funeral
before our gored feet.
Drink until you are drunk
but guide us home.

      Though the end should come last,
      ours is coming now —
      we are the drifting leaves
      in the cast of wind,
      trembling,
      unable to follow our repulsive skeletons
      over the narrow corners.
Kill us with bullets
or guide us home.

      Sharp saws roll and bang,
      chewing into a thousand us;
      their bellies are swollen
      full of our juicy bones,
there is nothing left of us.
Unleash our spirits
and guide us home.

I see ourselves,
crawling in *their* white plates
they hold forks,
dragging our lungs along
from table to table.
The end is around our necks,
put the plates aside
and guide us home.

July 20, 2018
Cisarua, Bogor Indonesia

Sighs of despair

Freedom seems beautiful
but I'm not free —
not even allowed to fantasise it.

I have the independent will to fly
but the weight
         of
            chains
               pulls
                  me
                     down.

If I could strip these chains
off my feet,
these shackles
off my neck,
undo
the back-to-back pains,
                  I would run away,
far from this
darkness,
despair
and solitude.

I would disappear
far from this scary cage
which they call '*my home*'.

I want to breathe
                    the fair and fresh air,
        take my stolen wings back,
            soar high —
            no more curfew;
            be free.

Help me unpause the time,
my aged mother is counting it;
the finest Seasons of tomorrow
await too.

Set me free,
to harvest more of tomorrows,
discover a new life,
explore another beginning.

Stop tearing away
what remains of me.

Set me free
and I will reclaim myself,
re-join my own being.

Set me free
to celebrate
my actual existence
or
grant me 'one more chance'
to gasp for a last breath.

January 01, 2020
Jakarta, Indonesia

Give back his stolen wages

A nine-year-old child,
abandoned in a lonely street
in the heat of the Sun.

He shivers in fear,
wrapped in torn rags
as the cold rain rages.

The hands pretending to provide shelter,
have taken his wages in bags
and evacuated
uncle George and Sir John —
Ibu Elizabeth on board to Bali;
Bapak Euro on vacation to Lombok.

He rumbles around with parched lips
but streams of kindness are withered;
the pool of compassion has gone dry.

He drags his ruins on
in long pauses,
anxiously rubs his decaying hands —
rocks against the bricks.

He must be searching for mercy
but they have murdered it
long time ago.

His childhood breaks
as the black shadow reaches,
clutching him tight
like a haunting ghost.

His sunken eyes explode storms of rain,
hunger and exhaustion leave him
frozen and sleepless.

You,
who have stolen his wages,
please return
for thoughts of death are emerging
like the swirling cloud in his head
as you lie there eating *kacang mede*[1].

April 23, 2016
Cisarua, Bogor, Indonesia

———

1. *Kacang mede*: Cashew in Bahasa Indonesia.

In red rifts of a thousand sighs

For the children of my homeland, Afghanistan

From the grasp of mountain breast;
garden of rare roses,
    clear rills of musky scents
    flourish
       down
         the cities of God —

lilac labour of laughter;
cheerful charm of joy
fill cups of your life
and make you whole.

My share,
    piles of pallid ribs,
    echoes of muffled children
    with bruised eyeballs,
    hanging on void cheeks,
cut and gore —
scenes unnoticed.

Pools of purple salt,
sleeping round my red chest —
sighs unheard.

Plots of brief flowers,
scattered in the haze of gunpowder
with petals lolled
upon their fractured lips —
sites unseen.

Buckets of worn-out shoes,
filling folders of flesh;
castles of fractured skulls,
lying cold on butchers' tables —
bones unburied.

Lonely graves in the shade of rocks
with swaying flags on missing epitaphs,
gasping for a familiar air
with yearning mouths —
graves unvisited.

Whispers of weeping mothers
echoing through the sea tides;
fathers' silent hours of fading
beyond the bitter borders of separation —
lives lost untold.

I, who write about this secret,
noticed
heard
saw
visited
told and lived them all
        with every grief
        that choked me up.

I, who noticed,
        mourn in the dusk;
        trace in the cannon of time
        echoes of my silenced screams.

I, who heard,
        wait in the red reefs of gardens,
        gasping IN
        the longing ashes of my stolen youth,
        scattered across the heat of fences,
        empty chairs and deserts of skulls.

I, who saw,
        hold in hand a pouch
        extracted from the depth of my chest,
        seek charity of ease from oceans
        whose tides are familiar
        to my sudden outburst sighs.

/...

I, who buried my own heart,
        fill in the pen
        with blood from my fingertips
        so the words I form never fade;
        are strong enough
        to turn into heavy snowflakes
        and pour over those known
        and unknown fortresses,
            built on the eyelashes of God
                to keep the sunshine
                    off my face.

I, who visited my own grave,
        hold a lantern,
        walking in the world of steel;
        in loneliness
        to find my other stolen half;

        prepare a farewell feast
        to bury it under the shade of almond trees
        and install a marble epitaph,
        inscribed with Hazaragi alphabets.

I, who uncensored their grief,
        collate a bridge
        between two worlds:
        imperious beetle bugs
        and pawned butterflies
        to transcend their light
        and craft brittle brushes
        from my hair
        to clean the flakes of sorrow
        off their delicate wings;
pull the bullets from their arteries
and wash the salty dust of separation
from their wounded cheeks.

October 18, 2021
Pajajaran, Bogor, Indonesia

Wounds have eyes

Nightmares unwrap
the past journal of traumas —
each event comes back
like a horrific movie scene
and smoke of burnt corpses
rises high,
leaping against the heavens.

I crash against tug-of-wars,
relentless in their strikes
against the gory sides of roads,
pitying for themselves.

The silent *Rubab*[1] stands oblivious
waiting in vain
for a voice to accompany;
my violin lays endlessly mute —
a dry piece of wood.

Eyes pour tears,
fragments of my heart
out my chin;
each droplet contains a name,
an image,
invisible to you.

Heart pangs;
breathing slows down,
reduces to final gasps
and death's touch
rises through flames,
burning it by my throat.

/...

I gather myself up,
sew all my bits back,
each time
I utter
a
single
word.

I'm done chopping
upon my torn chest —

the abundance of foretime,

a meal for you.

November 05, 2020
Jakarta, Indonesia

---

1. *Rubab*: A lute-like musical instrument originating from central
   Afghanistan — one of the two national instruments of Afghanistan.

Counting the time backwards

Anguish for fallen life,
threads of heart stretched out
as my soul lays on wrinkled papyrus
to entertain you with another elegy.

Past traces cleave in
like shattering blades of swords,
unzipping the fatal fist of old wounds,
fresh as yesterdays.

Head revolves around events,
fractions of death
Uncounted —

words, bulks of fire;
lungs choke upon my own flames —
ashes

un-moaned.

The cage is too small to move,
cold hands wave to the iron walls;
I collide against the rusting bars —
voice shivers
in my choked-out throat
as though it is no longer mine.

Solitude swiftly rears up,
mixed with smoke and wafts high
on the frayed edges of my heart,
pulling at its strings

/...

and music of grief echoes;
   curtain of thick shadows
    covers the infinite galaxies
in my eyes —
dead gaze suspended upon my breast,
counting to the ageing sighs of the sea.

January 09, 2018
Cisarua, Bogor, Indonesia

Piles of funerals

Grey pool of grief sighs low
and the heart bleeds syrup of red,
sweeping, floating dead-like,
abandoned far and wide.

My chest feels nothing
except the excruciating firestorms,
crushing right, left
from the hills of agonies
and melt lungs to ashes.

My head is a bank of hidden scars,
a clock, counting the track of terror —
red, grey and yellow.

When the alarm rings,
saddened gales of fear explode,
forming in me
rigid streams of torment —

noiselessly passing on to me
with handfuls of blasted hearts,
burned out skulls —
unrecognisable.

The afflictions,
camped upon my chest
are unbearable;
the deep cuts in my veins
are piles of funerals
with no bandage.

They are never measured
and shall never be.

/...

The grief spreads beyond my width.
It is not too far
nor within the reach.

September 04, 2020
Jakarta, Indonesia

Death lurks

Night, the cannon cloud,
                    rolling upon
                    our staggered souls;
            stillness runs life
            with despair
        and the ghostly shadow swirls in,
cold
uncaring.

        Bedding far beyond humble,
        far less than a rug
        to wrap my frozen soul in
        against the moaning thunders
        with wistful rain of blood.

        Frosty tiles,
        to lay my frozen ribs on,
        my torn backpack,
                    a pillow to rest my head upon.

        Bitter coldness breaches through,
    surges in and smites me sore;
        I shiver, lying bent
        upon my stiffened stomach
        with weak and shaking breath,
    mourning over my own miseries
    and unreturnable losses.

/...

Eyes are wide open —
two distant shores
stuck in swelling storms;
arms around my torso,
embracing the burden
of my ruptured world.

I draw my breath still,
squeezing myself
into a tight ball,
trying to ease the flamboyant fever
that rolls through me dirge-like.

Tips of sharp knives keep scratching,
digging through my hollowed-out stomach —
writhing pains
                        across my thinned body,
torment
            jolting me
                        awake.

I groan,
Crawl —
invisible needles crack through bones,
desolate sweat rushes
and darkness moans.

Food,
clean water scarce;
this frail body
                        far too thin to move
only salted tears left to swallow,

rotten carrots to chew
and poisoned water
 to get me through.

No one to hold my hand,
no energy left to stand —
welled-up eyes;
a few drops of mist
 alone to roll down,
 offering company.

No human voice do I hear,
nor a lullaby
except the distant frogs,
crying into the fist of this hostile night
and the gentle waves of nostalgia
that make their way into my heart.

Heartbeat hastens
like thunder strikes
as fear of death lurks in,
 hugging the rug of
 a misty soul.

August 09, 2018
Cisarua, Bogor, Indonesia

Jars of grief

Head,
a funeral
to the left-overs of past,
     heart hangs
           beating,
        breath tangled
        by the dark web of terror.

     Ears suckled
        to echoes of loud screams,
        ringing in
        sharp as arrows,
        cutting
           limb
               by
                  limb.

    When I shut my eyes,
I see debris of bodies
steeped in boiling blood,

        fragments of wrinkled,
        smoked out flesh,
        necklace the nearby trees.

Blasted legs,
    broken arms;
    worn-out heads,
laying here and there
on pond and ditches —

    vision
        fades
            away.

The smashed skulls;
sliced off throats
drowned in dirt and rubble —

that girl with a book,
burned on her exploded chest,
boy with eyes fixed
on the shadows of flame,
swirling above —

or the living corpses,
carrying the dead bodies
of brothers on shoulders,
mourning their hearts out.

I close my mouth,
burning smell of flesh
invades my whole being,
filling me up —
tips of knives
scratch the bones.

Everything slips from mind;
rigid winds of traumas
freeze the life's light
off my eyes —

all I see is a door,
leading into an old castle,
dark and dreary
with rusting iron bars
that are cold and eerie.

I press the jars of grief
against my shaking chest,
breathing in
every last drop of
hell's burning fires.

/...

I lay numb,
steeped in cold sweat;
deep drilling pain scatters,
breaching every nerve and vein —
stomach burns,
swollen

each time I write

or talk about my past.

December 14, 2017
Cisarua, Bogor, Indonesia

Exhume the light

I can no longer feel the glory of joy
nor can I sense the cusp of sorrow.

I've grown numb to all;
stranger to myself.

Smiles take more effort
to compose a melody of life;
laughter grew tired,
costs more tears
than cry itself.

Each attempt at laughter
feels like someone is pulling
my lungs
out of my stomach.

These eyes once beamed with passion,
turned into inescapable currents of flood.

You will drown in tears
if you look into them
from a closer distance.

Therefore, I dried them;
it took me a while to clean them up
from the stretched-out corners
in my wrinkles.

Maybe I haven't yet fully died.
I'm not fully alive either.

December 06, 2017
Cisarua, Bogor, Indonesia

A multitude of ruins

Early childhood dew parted
in Dahmardah and Tehran;
adulthood light struck off
in Quetta and Kabul;
youthful passion
swallowed by moist camps
in Bogor and Jakarta.

Here I'm now
                    far
                    out
hands,
empty as your barren eyes,
sinking in swarms of grief.

I carry forth
multitudes of my own ruins
on six split shoulders

to bury
among the wild trees,
standing as barriers
between I and life.

How should I greet
If I meet THEM alone?

June 07, 2016
Cisarua, Bogor, Indonesia

146

Don't ask why I don't smile

I became a father,
cried for my son;
the son became a father,
cried for his child.

I became a mother,
cried for my daughter;
the daughter became a mother,
cried for everyone.

I rushed to embrace my child
but grasped bloody scarves
and half-burned shoes —

the steady moon
and life itself cried.

Todays, tomorrows —
all passed on foggy highways,
the pleading visions
gazing at every door and window
glazed over —

the storms and highways cried.

No soil is unfamiliar to Afghanistani bones,
no foreign camp rejects our blood —

the silent walls,
and the unlived years cried.

Our rushing footprints
etched into every rock —

the numb mountains
and curved valleys cried.

Every border knows our names,
every patrolling officer beholds our faces,
every UN office memorised our numbers —

/...

the heartless silence,
and inhumanity cried.

Earth declined to enclose our eyes,
communities stood tall,
watched us,
melting in the flames of hatred —

the nearby flowers
and embracing sawgrass cried.

I stood before God for supplication,
to my shaking heart, shivering legs —

angels at dawn,
and Firaun[1] at sundown cried.

Buddhas from temples,
Jesus from churches,
creatures from seas,
birds from skies —

Muhammad[2] in Laylat al-Qadr[3] and Shimr[4] himself
at Karbala cried —

only the believers and ourselves didn't cry.

Don't ask how I feel, my beloved mother,
the cold rocks and rivers cry.

August 29, 2021
Pajajaran, Bogor, Indonesia

———

1. *Firaun*: The arrogant man, anyone inordinately proud, insolent, or unbelieving. Pharaoh, ancient title for Egyptian emperors.
2. *Muhammad* (PUBH): The prophet, Messenger of God.
3. *Laylat al-Qadr*: The Night of Power is, in Islamic belief, the night when Quran was first sent down from Heaven to the world and also the night when the first verses of the Quran were revealed to the Islamic prophet Muhammad. This night is described as better than a thousand months of worshipping.
4. *Shimr*: An Arab military commander from Kufa who martyred Husayn ibn Ali, the grandson of prophet Muhammad (PBUH), peace be upon him.

I've exhausted the universe

Pain and grief
      reached my ribs;
silence grew in me
tall as my height.

My heart has crushed
      to fine grinded ash,
soul hammered down,
mirroring the befallen
image of Buddhas
      off its glorious throne.

Worries lay next to me,
dining with me a meal
      that is grief.

They stand void and voiceless,
      exceeding the Puncak mountains;
dive deep in my veins —
into the fathomless
      depth of the Tasman Sea.

I curl myself up into tight cloud,
turning into red drops of rain,
pouring down onto your rooftops,
playing a little sleep song
until I exhaust the universe.

I want a larger share
of my solitude from you,
the stranger's universe!

April 15, 2023
Wellington, Aotearoa
The end of another beginning

149

VI
I HAVE ROOTS /
IN THE SOIL THERE

من آنجا ریشــه در خاك دارم

To remove me from there
is to uproot the heart

"I Have Roots in the Soil There" is a Persian saying
that signifies the profound influence of my birthplace
where the landscape becomes an extension of myself.
It is a declaration that resonates with a deep-seated
longing for my connection and a yearning to trace
my lineage, finding solace in the heritage that resides
within the earth.

Castles of shadow

My story is measured
like the lines of
an ungrammatical sentence
repeatedly corrected
by nit-pickers and pedants,
firing back
at every word
I utter,
and truth gives causalities.

Their mouths are full of blaze,
teeth sharp as sharks' —
ready to rip the head
off my shoulders
and burn the rest of me
to ashes.

So, I keep silent,
shut my mouth up,
biting my lungs up
so as not to die.

I let the breath of silence
suckle your ears,
trails of burning oak
swirl up and swallow
the rooves of your eyes.

I let my sore soul rest,
my bleeding nails heal
to the swift light of my pen,
pouring all in its wakefulness

until that fair;
flourishing Spring

/...

breaks out with laughter
and casts aside
the spells of lingering stillness
that built upon my tongue
a thousand castles of shadow.

October 14, 2018
Cisarua, Bogor, Indonesia

Four walls make the man free

Their feet nailed on our throats,
blood-drenched, sleeves pulled up,
slicing every head
that the *Hazaragi* shoulders carry.

Freedom, the twisted lies,
rages of annihilation ignite,
burning the core existence of life
into high hills of skulls
to fuel their appetite.

Converging walls,
drawn closer against our chests
at every passing beat;
squeezing souls against the soil —
no air to breath,
no light to guide —
crumbled piles of unpaired jaws,
invisible to all
but ourselves.

No ground to let our feet,
no paper beholds our names —
we are outcaste
from the edge of the beginning
and pushed to the bottom of time —
our ashen eyes are turning
into flickering stars.

/...

The rug of union with God
is ripped from our souls,
Masjids, our cold coffins
in the war against His existence.

Book of justice is scribbled,
sick and paralysed —
a word game,
an illusion.

Gales of genocide
under twisted scripts
with false order,
annihilating a tribe
older than Buddhas of Bamiyan.

Valleys of life,
aromatic lands of apricots,
the Final Solution —
tongues sewn to our lungs
so truth falls into cool oblivion.

We are dispatched
into freshly dug graves —
in the thousands,
dozens and pairs.

6.5 million indigenous crowns
are molten to ashes,
bones to dust,
flesh to soil;
souls to the sky.

Half perishes
behind iron bars of cages
or in dark drowning seas,
the other half
sinks in dust across borderlands;
some are disappeared for years —
dead nor alive.

This 'fencing'
ensures silence;
blocks are well-ordered
and piled on the rest.

Shield of justice,
a leaking jar of honey —
a fishing diary on sale,
we didn't wish to buy
but to rewrite ourselves.

Let us not shut our minds
so darkness enshrouds
and perish beneath the unneutral demons
who bribe the unclean tongues
to speak against the unspoken law.

Let's collect our bones,
stitch back in place
our blasted flesh
and re-join the spirit
of *Hazaragi* legends

/...

at whose clattering thuds of feet
the dragons would think twice
before burning a bush.

LET US draw a road
for them to follow —
drums only produce sounds
when the hammers kiss them
on the cheeks.

October 23, 2017
Jakarta, Indonesia

Pairs of brilliance

Open your eyes
to the embrace of light;
shake the dust of colonisation
from your shoulders;
clean the codes and numbers
off your foreheads —

let there be only more,
little meant wickedness
and less left you hostage.

Your heart,
too young to rust away
at the shared discount of pencils.

Be weighted;
brush the rashes
off your wrung skin,
the fainting frost
off your stalked cheeks.

You are no longer the befallen sight
but the whole,
tall and tailored
the chosen star —
the glimmering sun in rise,
pairing with the delight
of the morning breeze.

He created you
with love and patience
you belong and relate
to all time
and spaces.

/...

Get rearranged.
Pull yourself up.
Dive with the ocean
and let the sea be you.

Be unreachable.
to blindness.
ears filled with mud and salt.
to those who plucked
roses off your fragrant hair
and sold your numb skull —
to those
who pulled your nails off
and locked you up
in the darkness,
equivalent
to those of tombs.

Be un-bargainable
except to the unaided Creator.
un-replaceable
except with the Observer
of your supplications.

Hard to debase
except by the Knower of secrets
and Reorganiser of names,
difficult to compare
except with the Healer of hearts.
impossible to forget
except the One without ending
and the Giver without temperament.

He is the shelter
to accommodate your torn soul
with what are missing
and taken from you away.

Let your brilliance stand out,
radiate in all ages and lands
you step in.

June 01, 2017
Cisarua, Bogor, Indonesia

We are the history

Now that the wheel of politics extends,
we, the prisoners in moist islands,
turn into history —
     a history that becomes legends,
legends on demand for trade?

Legends of light,
        imprisoned to a final solution?

    In mountains of haze,
          called the white offshores
         by those
      who pluck hopes from the path to life
   to drip red down,
    pale grey tower drains?

Woe to those who scare the light,
    a sad reputation on its way
       for vile secrets are softly hidden
Courtesy to history
Long live the legends.

        Mysterious legend of myth,
      symbolic of light,
       Daud's shepherds —
   Metaphorical,
     Inspiring the moons
     to expand against wolves,
     eating the sun;
uplifting the sick valleys
     on bare cheeks to keep on the light
so pigs stop drinking our fading light.

    We are masters of patience,
      Daud tribes —
champions on our way home,

the flash lights drum up
our thunderous music of freedom,
the horizon rolls in joyful wails
of the free land,
                awaiting to host the fragrant figs.

A refugee woman measures it well
how light and shadow velveteen.

So beware,
her white veil shivers.

In death,
we blossom with flowers of light
    from whence we come,
    people are fully aware
                and murmur
                our unbeatable spirits,

        pure, noble sights
of ancient archaeologies,
teaching stones to speak in rhymes.

Cheers to a cup of hot Chai!

January 06, 2022
Pajajaran, Bogor, Indonesia

I am but more than a refugee

I am but
>   a poet,
>   harvesting in the garden of Ghazals,
>   a guide to the tossed vapor of noises
>>   unheard,
>   the blooming sea of awakening dreams,
>   the ultimate sense of life and joy,
>   reciting again the tongues of youth.

I am but
>   the certifying seed,
>   well-sown,
>   dancing to the trumpet of truth —
>   the interpreter of that vast sight
>   where man has never attempted to tread.

I am but
>   a divine and a high-ranking orchard place
>   where Spring forever resides,
>   wild roses never wilt
>   and grass never turns pale.

>   *Their* stone-walls and tall towers
>   shall not imprison my mind
>   nor will this physical confinement
>   or exile.

>   I roar against *their* incarcerating walls
>   and each echo is a rhythm in itself;
>   every thought cultivates
>   fine jewels of wisdom,

verses of Jalāl Ud-Dīn Muhammad Rūmī Balkhi
>>>   run wild in me.

I am but

the humbled servant of humans
never kowtowing to those greedy demons
who hold children of God behind iron bars
to enhance investment with hidden codes.

I am but

the new-born essence of Khushal Khattak,
a poet who sweated blood
until poetry became his name;
the extended verses of Mīr 'Alisher
'A pippin from an orchard on a farm in Kent.'

I am but

a jingle of keys to the bed-welded locks;
words with tough skin - ·
the hidden beauty,
forming Ahmad Shah's vision,
'I forget the throne of Delhi
when I remember the mountain tops
of my Afghan land.'

Wasef Bakhtari is my identity,
nurtured by Mahmud Tarzi's loving masterpiece
with his delusions, conjuring illusions in me.

I am but

the yearning blossom of *Ostai*.
the East — West — South — North,
lost to be found.

I am but

the re-incarnation, exalted forth
through reshuffling pages of history
and soon to be spoken aloud.

/...

I am but
      the harbinger of dead voices,
      the carrier of dead sighs,
      magically reshaping the seeds,
      ready to sprout in new generations.

      I summon Khalilullah Khalili's song,
      'I want nature to dominate,
      joy to dominate,
      laughter to dominate.'

I am but
      a pure nature,
      beholding the visage of God in it.
      I speak to trees,
      cry with roaring seas,
      smile with flowers
      and sing with the zephyr.

      Earth is my king-sized home,
      valleys my chest,
      mountains my shoulders;
      hillsides my forehead.

      I sit hunched in grief
      cold in the fading snow
      over polluted rivers
      and wear a shroud of white
      to mourn over
      the early death of fish.

I am but
      that wistful blossom of light,
      reflecting all colours;
      the sophisticated pen of Gul Pacha Ulfat,
      who carried the sun with him —
      the motion,
      bearing forth the sweet gift
      of lilacs' scent.

I am but
    the imminent arrival of all Seasons,
    the mesmerizing Spring,
    the harvested Summer,
    the purpled Autumn,
    the herald of Winter —

        I am that fine morning zephyr,
        emitting the reviving aroma of summer;
    sparrows take flight in my laughter
    and butterflies emerge from their cocoons
    at my arrival!

    My palms, the infinite Sufra
    of Kazemi's reviving stanza,
    the well-versed albums of Raziq Faani,
    the two splendid visions of Ismael Balkhi,
    softened by the heartfelt sonnets
    of Mohsin Changezi.

I am but
    the re-emerging strength
    of Kamran Mir Hazara,
    the well-flourishing dreams
    of *Ammi* and *Baba*
    and the careful sower of seeds,
    a-soon to yield
    to the raindrop of Spring.

I am but
    that fine Hirati saffron ink,
    painting the unfinished arteries
    of Faiz Mohammad Katibs,
    accompanied by the cool-breathed tone
    of Chang and Tanbur
    that Amir Khusro Balkhi linked his nerves with
    and the extracted bits of *Hazaragi* remnant,
    from Ghoriyan to Zabulian.

/...

I am but
      a tuneful flute from Ney,
      knower of unknown tunes;
      singer of unrhymed songs.

      My fingers are
      the strings of Egyptian Oud,
      dancing in unison,
      bouncing with delight
      forming music from nothing.

I am but
      the everlasting song of heavens,
      a *Hazaragi* Dambura,
      the verbal testimony of ancient art
      which converses with sun notes,
      portraying melodies of Ali Baba Taj.

I am but
      Shahid Balkhi's literary work,
      the well-woven circles of words;
      the wave of Sultani Ali Kishtman's tempo
      and the vitreous pour
      of Majrūh's lyrics.

I am but
      a journalist,
      the lord of my own words,
      giving volumes to moral
      and righteous voices
      which carry the truthful
      hymns of the voiceless.

I am engaged,
remain curious,
firm
and utterly prepared.

Because,
I am more than a
refugee.

December 17, 2020
Pajajaran, Bogor, Indonesia

———————

Afterword
Behrouz Boochani

Open your eyes to the embrace of light;
shake the dust of colonisation from your shoulders;
clean the codes and numbers off your foreheads.
— Abdul Samad Haidari, *Pairs of brilliance* (p.153).

Abdul Samad's poetry reaches new heights, going beyond his Hazara identity and statelessness. The poems embody the collective human struggle and the indomitable spirit his tribe has carried for generations against discrimination and genocide. His sharp pen crafts verses that reflect the ever-shifting landscape of truth, casting light into the shadows of events to reveal the hidden threads that weave our world's narrative.

Abdul Samad introduces a unique perspective on politics, colonialism, humanity, life and identity. His words carry the weight of profound grief, mourning altitudes of tragedy and displacement. Yet, this does not mean he writes as a victim but rather as an unbeatable advocate. What holds significant importance is his ability to intertwine these multifaceted layers within his literary work, displaying firm resistance for his unshakable convictions.

Excruciating anguish and separation embody the very soul of his verses, as he pens, "Pain and grief reached my ribs." Abdul Samad employs these elements within the context of resistance and struggle. He declares with courage, "I am not uprooted, nor silenced. I exist fully." This line represents his profound ontological understanding of his obligation as a Hazara, a refugee, journalist and, beyond that, as a human and a poet in this world.

This sentiment, "My soul stands instead of me" echoes throughout the pages of this book in woven metaphors, highlighting his Hazaragi strength in fighting for his identity and values.

What resonates with me the most in his poetry is not just how he employs words to challenge a system designed to oppress, strip away his identity and dignity; it's how he creates beauty within the context of tragedy, symbolising strength and inspiring empowerment for resistance.

Acknowledgments

This book is dedicated to my respected grandfather, Malik Ghulam Haidar Khan, my beloved grandmother, Mahi Jan Malik Haidar Khan, my strong and exalted father, Malik Yazdan Haidari, my courageous and kind-hearted mother, Amir Bigum Haidari and all my vibrant siblings whose unconditional love enriched my existence.

This book is the fruition of my great grandparents', my father's and my mother's teachings, love, support, guidance and prayers. Their teachings became the bedrock of my resilience, helping me withstand the torment years of imprisonment and endure the heavy weight of separation and injustice for almost a decade. My father carried the whole sun with him, enlightening my heart with the virtues of truthfulness, justice, tolerance, helpfulness, compassion, strength and kindness towards all beings.

To my beloved family, I apologise for being physically distant from you over the past ten years when you needed me the most. If only circumstances had allowed, I would have chosen to be by your side, but the vastness of this world has confined me within iron walls. I am deeply sorry for any pain my absence has caused and I hope you can find it in your hearts to forgive me.

My heartfelt gratitude goes out to my foster parents, Dr Te Manawa Murray Dunn and Her Excellency, Pam Dunn, the New Zealand High Commissioner to Malaysia and Brunei Darussalam. I am deeply thankful for your immense love and motivation which helped me overcome the feelings of darkness during the last five years. You have been the light guiding me to find the direction to home where my soul found comfort.

I extend my heartfelt gratitude to Lesmina Sari, my esteemed editor whose invaluable expertise and profound literary knowledge have shaped the cadences of my poems. Your intellectual wisdom and guidance remarkably refreshed and unfettered my thoughts in completing this book. These poems would not have found the comfort and strength they sought without your unique poetic sensibility. Your exceptional vision and academic insight put light to every verse and stanza and gave a breath to this book. You have been there when there was no one else, making sure I was nourished, cared for and found, stitching my wounds with the threads of mending love and kindness.

I am greatly indebted to my dearest friend, Kevin Yau Cheong, who embraced me and many others like a brother. His patience and wisdom have added values to my resistance and literary work. I had not yet met him when he stepped forward showing excitement for *The Red Ribbon*. In that moment, his vibrant energy surpassed my own joy, as he fully celebrated the success of that book. To Ichi Lin, whom I had the privilege to meet through Mr Kevin. She has transcended the boundaries of ordinary nourishing and become not just a sustenance but also a symphony of inspiration, reminding me that with genuine love and kindness the universe becomes a garden of limitless possibilities. Ichi's humble attitude and compassionate heart that beats for everyone is like a Tawiz to wear. Kevin and Ichi are the two unspoken heroes whose extended hands pour life into the empty jars of those who have been forgotten in the dark corners of camps for over a decade.

To an endearing sister and family member, Amanda Damayanti. Her unconditional love and support nourished me like flawless water streams of Dahmardah. Mei Chou Donovan, the spouse of former U.S. Ambassador to Indonesia, His Excellency, Mr Joseph R. Donovan Jr; His Excellency, Mr Ambassador Rudrendra

Tandon, who liberated my identity; my kind-hearted friend, Mr Edward Davies, the Southeast Asia News Editor for Reuters and the current president of The Jakarta Foreign Correspondents Club for his enthusiastic support and unwavering belief in my work. Thank you for taking me where you thought I belonged, the JFCC community.

I also cherish the love and support from my dearest friends Chris Gee and Vidya McSingh. With their guidance and love, I have begun to realise the meaning of my existence. With them I feel the essence of familyhood. My humble gratitude to Amanda Calder for her unconditional support to make sure I flew through the cadence of clouds safely to my new home, Aotearoa New Zealand where the glad landscapes speak with God and the reviving fragrance of oceans clears the lungs. To PEN International, particularly Ross Holder, to you, I dedicate the lights of my lyrics.

I would also like to extend my warmest gratitude to FCCANZ (Foreign Correspondents' Club Aotearoa New Zealand) for their earnest and exceptional support upon my arrival in Wellington. My utmost gratitude to the New Zealand government for holding the light before my beclouded path to guide me home — particularly the Associate Minister for Immigration, Mr Hon Phil Twyford. I am eternally grateful to the New Zealand Ministry of Social Development (MSD) for all the nurturing support you poured before me as a newly arrived former refugee with nothing but empty hands.

I would also like to extend my gratitude to Mr Hassan Rateq for his invaluable contributions to the refinement of the Dari text, which added a touch of literary brilliance to the work.

My deepest gratitude extends to all who have recognised my struggles, offered healing hands, uplifted my spirit along my winding journey and have expressed their good will without me knowing. Your presence glistened in the depths of the unknown.

The completion of *The Unsent Condolences* would not have been possible without the support and assistance of you who cannot be named here. To each and every one of you, I owe the realisation and fruition of my poems.

Abdul Samad Haidari

July 23
Wellington, Aotearoa/New Zealand

Printed in the USA
CPSIA information can be obtained
at www.ICGtesting.com
LVHW041107230324
775320LV00006B/600